Praise for
DIVINE DESTINY

"If you like to be inspired through scriptures and stories, *Divine Destiny* is a daily devotional that will help you go deeper in your relationship with God."

—Alex Kendrick,
Actor and director of COURAGEOUS,
WAR ROOM, OVERCOMER

"*Divine Destiny* is not just a daily read—it will inspire you to live a lifestyle in worship. Filled with powerful scriptures, inspiring stories, practical examples, and thoughtful questions, this devotional will effortlessly shift you into the God zone. *Divine Destiny* will warm your heart and elevate you to deeper connection with Christ."

—Mindy Rosser,
Sheraton Kauai Resort, event manager

"In the NBA, one of the highest compliments a player could have among his peers was "Game knows Game." *Divine Destiny's* GOT GAME—it carries about it a spirit of excellence and will help you blaze a trail toward God's destiny for you. This devotional is written with the precision of a surgeon, wisdom of an elder, and compassion of a rescuer. Enjoy the journey."

—Adrian Branch,
World Champion LA Lakers, college basketball analyst,
Certified Life Coach

"Once again, Scott delivers a masterful piece of art in *Divine Destiny*. Like a masterful painter, Scott pulls colorful stories and principles from Scripture to help teach us in everyday practical living. Each day will bring you a rich new perspective, so you may grow and mature in your walk of faith."

—Donna Johnson,
Entrepreneur and author of
My Mentor Walks on Water

"This 31-day devotional will give you a picture of how God sees your destiny. Scott biblically illustrates what God thinks and how He thinks so you can connect the dots between today and God's best future for you."

—Tim Elmore,
Author, speaker, founder of
Growing Leaders

"*Divine Destiny* offers profound insight and practical guidance for spiritual growth and leadership principles. What an amazing tool for everyday inspiration, especially for the workplace believers."

—Angel Barnett,
CEO of Dream Institute

"*Divine Destiny* is a book—really a GUIDEBOOK—to provide you a map for an abundant life in your Jesus journey. Don't just read it; pray through it, digest it, and put its Biblical principles to work in your life. You'll be glad you did."

—Jeff Rogers,
Chair of Park Place & OneAccord,
Founder KIROS

"The intention of a devotional book is to turn your heart toward God and inspire your thoughts. It opens your mind to a new and richer perspective on life. Scott Hogle achieved that with *Divine Destiny* and has taken it a step further. You will not only be inspired to see God's hand at work in your life, but you will also know He has been continually guiding you toward your Divine calling. You will be affirmed that you are doing exactly what God has called you to do. Be blessed! Read *Divine Destiny*!"

—**Karen Moore,**
Devotional book author & speaker

"*Divine Destiny* points the way to living an empowered, supernatural life so you can accomplish all God has purposed for you to do. If you're looking to bring the power of God into your profession, *Divine Destiny* will help you to uncover and unlock all God has prepared for you."

—**Tom Ziglar,**
CEO, Ziglar, Inc., and
proud son of Zig Ziglar

"Few pastors and Christian leaders really understand 'marketplace ministry' or how to deal with a business leader who feels a powerful and passionate desire to share their faith walk through their everyday career experiences. But that's exactly where Scott Hogle is at his best. From being a successful business leader to helping raise up an entire generation of marketplace leaders, Scott thrives at the intersection of faith, business, and leadership. And now, his new devotional, *Divine Destiny*, takes that calling to an entirely new level by demonstrating how you, too, can live an inspired Christlike walk in the marketplace. This is the book for anyone who feels God has called him or her to the business world. It will inspire you, motivate you, and give you a new perspective you never knew existed."

—**Phil Cooke, Ph.D.,**
Filmmaker, media consultant,
and author of *Church on Trial:*
How to Protect your Congregation, Mission,
and Reputation During a Crisis

"Scott Hogle has written some of the most inspirational paragraphs I've ever read. Now, Scott's done it again with the latest in the Divine Series: *Divine Destiny*…a 31-day devotional to put the Real You back in action. If your spiritual energy is running on empty, a few minutes in the morning with *Divine Destiny* will fill your tank to live inspired for the day."

—**Michael W. Perry,**
Mornings on America's highest-rated adult
contemporary radio station—KSSK

"*Divine Destiny* is an inspiring treasure chest of devotions and testimonies that bring God's word to life, His will, and His way. It's an incredible journey of discovering and discerning God's purpose and calling on our lives through the transformational life lessons of everyday people. It's a lifeline of God stories captured in a rich and heartfelt literary legacy."

—**John Tilton,**
President and senior pastor,
New Hope O'ahu.

"There's MORE God wants to do with you and for you in your walk with Jesus. *Divine Destiny* will enlighten the eyes of your heart to discover, then move in your true eternal purpose, your spiritual 'In Christ' superpowers, and reveal His assignment in this season of your life."

—Yvonne Yanagihara,
Market enablement manager Hawaii,
Spectrum Enterprise

"Coupling broad principles and concepts from the Bible with stories and illustrations drawn from his experience as a leader, father, husband, and friend, Scott Hogle provides believers with insightful and practical ways to discern their path forward."

—Abdu Murray,
President of Embrace the Truth and author

"Experience the divine power of discovering your personal vision and purpose with this exhilarating book, *Divine Destiny*. Scott Hogle, a prolific author who has a deep understanding of spiritual growth and personal development, guides you on this extraordinary journey. 'Let God cast His vision across the screen of your imagination and watch it incubate in your spirit.' Can you imagine seeing your ideal goals and dreams take place before they actually happen? What if you developed your imagination for the glory of God so that his kingdom is increased? Scott Hogle, in his book *Divine Destiny*, shows you how to do just that. Let this book be the catalyst for your journey of faith."

—Dr. Lori Salierno-Maldonado,
CEO, Teach One to Lead One

"God has given Scott the mind and courage of Daniel. You will see this demonstrated throughout the pages of *Divine Destiny*. This pioneering devotional will show you how to combine your marketplace and ministry callings."

—Wayne Cordeiro,
Senior pastor & president, New Hope International

"In this 31-day devotional, *Divine Destiny* offers readers the opportunity to renew their mind with God's wisdom and revelation in a way that combines their daily walk with their devotion to God."

—Craig Pankow,
President, Pacific Rim Christian University

"*Divine Destiny* is brilliantly crafted to inspire hope, faith, and trust in Christ. This book will stretch your mindset to reveal your true purpose and take your walk with God to higher ground."

—Rusty Komori,
Bestselling author

"As a Bible teacher and seasoned people-developer, I find Scott Hogel's newest book, *Divine Destiny*, an exciting read that reveals the hand of God working in the most extraordinary way through ordinary people. In this daily devotional, you will receive a divine deposit from the Holy Spirit to strengthen your intimacy with Him and direct your steps toward your high calling in Christ Jesus."

—Eileen Quinn, M.Ed.,
Public relations manager,
Andrew Wommack Ministries

"In my 50 years of walking with Jesus, I have read many devotional books, some by famous authors & preachers who at some point are scrambling for what could be called 'filler.' This is not the case in *Divine Destiny*. This 31-day devotional has a power-punched spiritual lesson in every chapter filled with biblical content and Spirit-led wisdom. *Divine Destiny* reminds us that though our final 'destination' is not until we get to heaven, there are many divine steps along the way revealing guideposts and spiritual food to find if we know what to look for. *Divine Destiny* will open your eyes to many hidden biblical truths. Scott quotes biblical characters (Boaz), giants of church history (John Wesley), and movie stars (Kevin Costner) while making generous uses of the metaphor (Boaz as a 'door opener'). We find him using his car as a metaphor for life, speaking about 'God Winks' on the freeway during a time of Windshield Worship that created a divine appointment with a teenage boy who needed help on the highway! *Divine Destiny* uses several creative ways to keep the reader locked in. It must be said, however, that you don't get the feeling that he is using his creativity for the sake of creativity but to make use of what I would call 'destiny doors,' where each chapter reveals to us God's creative portals into our own hearts."

—**Danny Lehmann,**
Director of University of the Nations,
Youth with a Mission KONA

DIVINE DESTINY

SCOTT HOGLE

Made for Success Publishing
www.MadeForSuccess.com

Distributed by Blackstone Publishing

First Printing
Library of Congress Cataloging-in-Publication data
Hogle, Scott
        Divine Destiny: Discover the Jesus Calling for Your Life:
            p. cm.

LCCN: 2024952471
ISBN: 978-1-64146-907-4 *(PBBK)*
ISBN: 978-1-64146-908-1 *(eBook)*
ISBN: 978-1-64146-909-8 *(AUDIO)*

Printed in the United States of America

For further information, contact Made for Success Publishing
+1425-526-6480 or email service@madeforsuccess.net

TABLE OF CONTENTS

ACKNOWLEDGMENTS

THANK YOU to the many family, friends, and mentors mentioned in *Divine Destiny*. As you've shared your God Stories with me, they have inspired me to draw closer to God. Your stories are now part of my story. While some of those mentioned in *Divine Destiny* are now in heaven, their stories live on as testimonies for eternity to proclaim the wonders and works of God. My hope for you, the reader, is that as you read my story and others in *Divine Destiny*, God speaks to you about your story. My prayer for you is that as you read the testimonies of those who have gone before you and those written about, God will birth a new story in your life. I can't wait to hear the new God Story He brings about in your life during this season of pursuit of your Divine Destiny.

FOREWORD

I have long believed that people represent individual pieces in God's divine jigsaw puzzle. Each of us is shaped differently, includes different colors, and plays different roles in the picture. Only when all the puzzle pieces are in the right place is the puzzle complete and can display the whole picture. I've found it difficult, however, to put a puzzle together without the box top that reveals what the picture of the jigsaw puzzle should look like when complete. In fact, if you're working with a 1,500-piece jigsaw puzzle, it's nearly impossible. Why? Because the box top provides the big picture.

In a very real sense, this is what Scott Hogle does for us in this book. He paints a series of pictures to help us identify and then walk in God's Divine Destiny for our lives.

As I read and reflected on the pages of this devotional guide, I kept thinking over and over that I was seeing the box top for what our Creator wants for us. I was seeing a blueprint for how our Father in Heaven wants us to perceive the world around us. Scott gives us the whole picture, showing us not merely what to think but how to think.

As I read each devotional, he continued to clarify how I (and we) should approach our careers, our income, our spouses, our families, our communities, and our relationship with God.

I'm not going to lie to you. In the world we currently live in, it's easy for me to become overwhelmed with the day-to-day grind. Beyond our crowded calendars, a person who's on social media is consuming an average of 10,000 messages each day. It's enough to put anyone in a self-protective mode, where we merely react to the noise and clutter of our days. It's understandable that we slip into survival mode. In this reality, we need others to offer us wake-up calls. We need people to equip us to live better, to help us shift back into the right gear, where we take the initiative. When we receive this, we relearn to play offense, rather than defense in our lives. We can live intentionally instead of reacting to our days.

Divine Destiny challenges us to live our best lives.

It will enable you to spot God's promptings on a busy day. It will empower you to turn a disadvantage into an advantage. It will clarify "God winks" in your life, helping you to see that what just happened to you may not have been a coincidence after all. It will provide you with a birds-eye view (or should I say a God's-eye view) of even the little activities you experience and the annoyances you endure each week. It will help you trust. It will help you become resilient. It will help you love.

I cherish it when I interact with a devotional guide that doesn't only make me feel better but makes me think better. That's what Scott Hogle will do for you in this volume. I suggest you take time each day (as I have done) to spend time with this book, writing down your own thoughts and processing your own applications to each chapter. Then, study the scripture that corresponds with each devotional. I think you're going to love the box top of God's jigsaw puzzle.

—Tim Elmore
Author, speaker, founder of Growing Leaders

INTRODUCTION

The time is NOW to live your DIVINE DESTINY! You are about to experience inspiring stories of everyday people who discovered their Divine Destiny, developed their spiritual strengths, and learned how to experience miracles in everyday life. This book is about how you can, too, one day at a time. You will hear how one woman turned a death sentence from a doctor into divine healing, how another turned barrenness into fruitfulness, and how God led another to find a husband. You will read how a mission to help others in crisis turned an act of obedience into a million-dollar return and how one man received a sure Word from God that launched him into a new career and calling. What God did for these saints, He can do for you. You will be inspired to turn your drive time into worship time, receive God winks and whispers, and be trained to tune your ear to hear God's voice. If you've ever desired to develop courage like Joshua, walk in your high calling like the Apostle Paul, or inquire of the Lord like David, you've found the right book. *Divine Destiny* will bring scripture to life in everyday situations so you can live supernaturally in today's modern world. How would your life be different if you could walk daily in the garden with God as Adam did? You can!

too will become a key participant in these last days. What is required of you? Learning to walk in the Divine Destiny God prepared for you before the foundation of the world (Ephesians 2:10). This daily devotional will change how you read the Bible, see yourself, relate to others and, most importantly, to God. After 31 days of experiencing God in a new way, you will find, follow, and fulfill God's purpose for your life. Let's get started!

JOURNAL YOUR DESTINY TODAY

> "God has chosen journaling to clarify through the pen
> what the Spirit has spoken." ~Scott Hogle

Questions are important to Jesus. When you ask him a question, your heart goes into a listening posture. In the Gospels, Jesus asked over 300 questions. Throughout the Old Testament, some of the most important conversations started with God asking questions. God asked Solomon, "What would you like me to do for you?" God asked Hagar, "Where have you come from, where are you going?" To Elijah, God asked, "What are you doing here?" God will ask you questions, and He likes it when you ask Him questions. Questions open the door to having a divine conversation. His desire is for a dialogue, not a monologue. Questions create conversations that lead to greater intimacy.

> *"Write the vision and make it plain on tablets,*
> *that they may run who read it."* Habakkuk 2:2

Write what you hear, perceive, or see! The following questions were written to help you discover your destiny for TODAY. None of us are promised tomorrow, but you can experience a perfect day by living in pursuit of God's Will. As you enter into devotional time with the Lord, He may lead you to develop new questions to help you draw nearer to Him. Here is one word of advice on how to receive from God when asking questions while in prayer: When you ask, listen intuitively for answers. What that means is that as you ask God a question, whatever you hear, perceive, or see in response, be sure to write it down. God may give you a picture, an idea, or bring a memory to mind. God's answer may not make sense in the moment but may be for an appointed time. Here are some questions to help you discover your destiny for today. Please personalize them or put them in the first person as the Lord leads you.

WHO

is God leading me to connect with today?

WHAT

is God prompting me to do?

WHERE

do I need to go to walk out today's assignment?

WHEN

is God's perfect timing?

WHY

might God be leading me in this direction?

Companion videos for *Divine Destiny* and a FREE *Divine Life Journal* can be found at www.ScottHogle.com

The High Calling

*"But this one thing I do, forgetting those things which are
behind, and reaching forth unto those things which are before,
I press toward the mark for the prize of the HIGH CALLING
of God in Christ Jesus"* Philippians 3:13-14 (KJV).

Do you know God's HIGH CALL for your life? The Apostle
Paul remarked, "I reach for the HIGH CALL in Christ
Jesus," signifying that there are various callings and sacrifices
that honor God. When you ask God what His HIGH CALLING
is for your life, He may give you an answer or present you with
options. God conversations can be a monologue from you or a
dialogue between you. Each person's HIGH CALLING will be
different as each has their own assignment. Some assignments
are short-term, others long-term. The HIGH CALL for your
life is God's Perfect Will for you in that season of your life.

THE THREE WILLS OF GOD

*"And do not be conformed to this world, but be transformed
by the renewing of your mind,
so that you may prove what the will of God is,
that which is good and acceptable and perfect."* Romans 12:2

I like to metaphorically think of the Three Wills of God as the
"good, acceptable, and perfect Will of God." The Apostle Paul
taught that there are multiple paths you can pursue in God's Will,
but there is one HIGH CALL: His PERFECT WILL for your life.

My friend Elieen was presented with a marriage proposal multiple times, which she kept turning down. She was undecided and felt she really needed a Word from God. She asked what He thought, and God said, "You don't have to marry him; I can bring you someone else. But marrying him is My best for you. Through your relationship with him, you will experience My best." If Elieen had chosen a different path, she would not have sinned; she would still be in the Will of God. But she desired God's Perfect Will, His best, and she would settle for nothing less. She is happily married today and experiencing God's best. Discovering God's HIGH CALLING and Perfect Will IN-SEASON, the season you are presently in, is essential for you to reach your Divine Destiny.

Here are three illustrations of different types of calling and how people discovered their HIGH CALLING in season.

THE COMMAND CALLING

"As they ministered to the Lord, and fasted, the Holy Ghost said, 'separate me Barnabas and Saul for the work whereunto I have called them.'" Acts 13:2

Has God ever SENT you somewhere or to someone? Paul and Barnabas were set apart and SENT to the Gentiles. When God calls you directly, this is a command call. There are many direct callings in the Bible where someone has been SENT. Jonah was sent to Nineveh to preach a message of repentance. Samuel was sent to David to anoint him as King. Elijah was sent to mentor Elisha as his replacement. Moses was sent to Egypt after forty years in the Midian desert to rescue Israel from slavery, and the list goes on. Have there been moments when God specifically directed you to go somewhere, reach out to someone, or take a particular action? A command call can be audible but is most likely an unmistakable word spoken deep in your spirit; it has an authoritative tone.

Embrace the "IN-BETWEEN" assignment, between being anointed and appointed for the Command Call. There is often a DIVINE TIME GAP between being anointed and appointed, between God's announcement to you and your assignment starting. David was anointed when he was about 15 years old, but he would not step into his destiny as king until he was 30. David spent fifteen years in preparation, his wilderness years, whereby God was working things behind the scenes, readying him for his Divine Destiny. God's Perfect Will for you may require seasons of transition and training. Eleven years would elapse between Paul's conversion experience on the Damascus Road when the Holy Spirit called him and Barnabas. Some biblical scholars believe the Apostle Paul spent three years in preparation in the Arabian desert, learning directly from the Lord before being commissioned as the Chief Evangelist to the Gentiles. Joseph spent thirteen years between the pit and palace before becoming Governor of Egypt—Joseph's training camp was servitude and prison in a foreign land, but God was with him every step of the way, blessing the work of his hands. Have you received a COMMAND CALL? This is God's HIGH CALL for you. If you are unsure, you may be in the "IN-BETWEEN," "IN-BETWEEN" the anointing and appointing. How would you describe the current season you are in?

Some COMMAND CALLS take years in the making but then appear in a Kairos moment. A Kairos moment is "the fleeting rightness of time," meaning you can miss God and what He has planned for the next leg of your destiny if you don't act when spoken to. TJ Malievsky left secular broadcasting to serve God in Christian Broadcasting, but he experienced an in-between time gap between his calling and his assignment. In his desert-type training season, TJ left an affluent lifestyle as a broadcast executive and worked as a carpet installer, struggling paycheck to paycheck. In his three-plus years of preparation between calling and assignment, he found himself out of touch with colleagues in broadcasting.

During a lunch break at a park, in between carpet jobs, God whispered to him, "Go home!"

TJ asked, "Why?"

God replied, "It's beginning."

Upon arriving home, the phone rang, and a man named Ed Marshak from Katz Media in New York was on the other line. Ed asked, "Where are you? No one can find you. Pat Robertson has been looking for you." Within a week, TJ was on a plane to interview and accept a job with the Christian Broadcast Network.

What was happening? TJ's "IN-BETWEEN" season of anointing and appointment was over; his season of training for the first leg in his calling was ending. TJ obeyed this COMMAND CALL, which would jump-start a life-long career as a Christian broadcaster. TJ's assignment included traveling the globe to open doors that would bring Christian TV programming to satellite and cable systems in international markets. TJ, the Apostle Paul, and Barnabas shared one thing when the COMMAND CALL came. They were seeking God and wanted God's HIGH CALL for their life. They left their old life behind and stayed in faith while waiting for God to open the door for their HIGH CALL. Have you been instructed by God directly or through someone else? If so, this is a COMMAND CALL.

THE OPEN-DOOR CALLING

"He who is holy, who is true, who has the key of David, who opens and no one will shut, and who shuts and no one opens, says this: 'I know your deeds. Behold, <u>I have put before you an open door</u> which no one can shut, because you have a little power, and have followed My word, and have not denied My name." Revelation 3:7-8

What door of opportunity is open for you? When I have multiple options in front of me, I pray and ask, "Dear Lord, please close the doors that are not of you."

Karen Moore was a middle-school teacher and was uncertain whether she'd have a job for the following year due to a reduction in staff. She set out to look for a job in a totally different industry. One day, Karen opened the Yellow Pages randomly and saw American Greetings at the top of the page. She wondered what credentials she might need to write for the company—having just completed a master's degree. When she reached American Greetings in Cleveland, Ohio, the administrative assistant was taking a break, and the head of HR picked up the phone. Karen talked with the woman for over an hour and was invited to interview for a job.

Karen didn't know then what she knows now: that her desire to find a new direction for her work would land her in the lane of her vocational calling. When Karen knocked on the door of American Greeting Cards, a door of opportunity opened for her that God would use to launch her into her Divine Destiny. God will use the needs and desires of your heart like He did Karen to direct your steps toward your Divine Destiny.

As it turned out, Karen had a knack for writing greeting cards and developing new ideas. That was 15,000 greeting cards and 130 books ago. Her spirit awakened as she walked through the door of opportunity. When she did, she landed on her calling.

Today, Karen brings joy to tens of thousands of people through her greeting cards, devotional books, and blogs shared around the world. Concerned she'd lose her teaching job, Karen looked for a totally new direction and found her calling. Like Karen, God may use a need in your life to drive you to seek a divine opportunity he has prepared just for you.

What doors of opportunity are open before you?

*"Coincidence for a Christian is God's providence
making itself known."* ~Scott Hogle

THE LOOK-SEE-DO CALLING

*"What you see and are sensitized to in your spirit is
God opening your spiritual eyes."*
~Scott Hogle

What has God opened your eyes to? Mike Hudgins, founding pastor of the Vineyard Community Church in Laguna Niguel, traveled to India and waited his turn in line to meet Mother Teresa. When his turn came to talk to her, he told her that he was a pastor and asked, "Is there anything you think I should be doing?"

Mother Teresa looked up at him and said, "LOOK - SEE - DO." She was communicating simply, "Find the hurting, then help them." Jesus told his disciples that when they helped someone in need, it was as if they were helping Jesus himself. Mother Teresa was saying the same thing. LOOK for the need, SEE the need, and then DO the good deed. When you do, you will have found Jesus. Mother Teresa spent a lifetime doing just that and instructed Mike to do the same.

Mike responded to her, "I live in Orange County where people have money, there does not seem to be much need there."

Mother Teresa responded, "You're wrong! There are people in need there, and you need to do something to help them." *It is amazing how your spirit can become sensitized to something when God puts it on your heart.*

Not long after Mike returned to Orange Country, my auntie Cecilia and her friend Jessica, who attended Mike's church, felt prompted to start a food pantry. They discussed the idea with Pastor Mike and he was in support. As the pantry grew, they suggested getting a separate building for the food ministry. Today, Mercy Warehouse has over 200 employees and volunteers, who feed over 1000 people a week. The need you are sensitized to is Jesus pointing the way; it is your LOOK-SEE-DO calling.

Mercy Warehouse not only helps people in need but also benefits those who volunteer, as helping others also helps oneself. By connecting volunteers with those in need, Mercy Warehouse has created a lasting and infinite impact. Is there a need around you where God may be calling you to serve "the least of these?"

*"You cannot serve another without making a deposit
into eternity for yourself." ~Scott Hogle*

Serving people in need is one of the ways in which God will invite you into His eternal work. Your LOOK-SEE-DO calling may come by way of a tug on your heart, a suggestion from the Lord, or a compassion you are feeling toward someone. The Apostle Paul saw a man in a dream from Macedonia waving him over to come and help him. Paul, knowing how God uses the LOOK-SEE-DO way of calling, changed his travel plans and traveled to Macedonia. He never met the man in the dream, but he did meet a woman named Lydia, who would become central to funding Gospel efforts in Europe. It's possible that your responding to God's LOOK-SEE-DO calling is His way of positioning you for your next assignment, anointing, or season of provision. What might God's LOOK-SEE-DO calling be for you right now?

*"And the King will answer and say to them, 'Truly I say to
you, to the extent that you did it for one of the least of these
brothers or sisters of Mine, you did it for Me.'"* Matthew 25:40

REFLECT TO CONNECT

1. What type of callings or assignments have you received?
2. In what direction is God leading you through desire, burden, or direct call?
3. What advice would you give to someone who is seeking God but finds themselves in an "in-between" season?

Mana

*"You created my inmost parts, you wove me in my mother's
womb, I am fearfully and wonderfully made. All of my days
were written in your book before one came to be"*
Ref. Psalm 139:14-17.

MANA, a Hawaiian term meaning spiritual or divine power, signifies the unique essence God gave you at birth. Each person receives a distinct part of His DNA, making you one of nearly eight billion individuals with a unique DNA fingerprint. You are wonderfully and perfectly made, endowed with special powers for His Divine Purposes. Before you were born, God determined your MANA, and it's up to you to discover and nurture it. As you develop your MANA, it grows and strengthens like a muscle. Your MANA might remain dormant for a time, only to be awakened in a moment of need. In times of challenge or crisis, your MANA can be ignited, propelling you toward your Divine Destiny.

WHO AM I, AND WHY AM I HERE?

*"Before I formed you in the womb I knew you,
And before you were born I consecrated you;
I have appointed you as a prophet to the nations."*
Jeremiah 1:5

Have you discovered your divine design? MANA is your natural gifting from God that He anoints. You may experience this anointing before coming to salvation or before discovering your purpose in life, but make no mistake, your MANA is pregnant with purpose. MANA is a clue to what you are designed to do, like a large breadcrumb that leads you to your Divine Destiny. To Jeremiah, God said, *"I knew you before you were formed in your mother's womb and I ordained you to be a prophet to the nations."* Have you discovered what your spiritual powers and purposes are? When your MANA is at work, you know it is God helping you. There is something about you that is MORE, in a way that transcends your natural abilities.

Your MANA may show up as a setback in life, something you were born with, or a set of circumstances that stacked the odds against you. God's specialty is hiding set-ups for success in a setback. To the Apostle Paul, He said, "In your weakness my power is made perfect."

He may also hide one of your superpowers as a handicap that He desires you to channel. I was diagnosed at a young age as Hyperkinetic, one who can't sit still and always needs to be busy. I learned how to harness this internal drive (God's wiring) to keep active by bending it into my day-to-day activities. This handicap has helped and allowed me to increase my productivity and prosperity in the lane I am called. What setback is God hiding in your stable of gifts? You have MANA yet undiscovered. God delights when you discover His design in you.

What's in your MANA Matrix? You will have multiple gifts that make up your MANA Matrix. Your key spiritual superpower(s) will work in conjunction to support your other giftings. One of my spiritual superpowers is a wordsmith. When I was in school, I did not excel in English or spelling class. But as I grew older and entered the business world, I realized I had to be able to speak and write with a degree of competence. As I worked on this, a strong desire for how to best say words and phrases the right way emerged. That desire was a key God used to unlock new MANA in me. As time passed, my desire continued to increase, and I became a craftsman of words. God gave me a gift of wordsmithing I did not have prior and then anointed that gift, which turned into a spiritual superpower and a core MANA strength of mine. This spiritual superpower feeds the other gifts in my MANA Matrix and causes them to blossom. Wherever there are "words at work" in my life, my MANA gift of wordsmithing comes alive. This gift feeds my day-to-day assignments in the areas of communicating, selling, leading, speaking, writing, and more. As you think about what's in your MANA Matrix, remember that gifts unlock in season, when put under demand, and come alive when you are working in your lane of assignment. Acquiring an awareness of how to spot emerging MANA in yourself and others is key to walking out your Divine Destiny. God has given you multiple gifts that make up your MANA Matrix. Here are a few clues to help you discover them.

7 SIGNS OF YOUR SPIRITUAL SUPERPOWER

"My grace is sufficient for you, for power is perfected in weakness." 2 Corinthians 12:9

1. **SUFFERING:** Pain may unlock or reveal your MANA. Mel Gibson's 2004 movie, *The Passion*, is about the suffering of Jesus for the sins of the world so you and I can be reconciled to the Father. PASSION means "The willingness to suffer for what you love." Is there a pain in your past that God is repurposing into a higher purpose? In the very thing you suffered, do you now have a PASSION to help others? This PASSION now unlocks MANA for your lane of calling. Adults who once were trapped in addiction or suffered abuse, now have a desire to help others break free from those circumstances. Is there a cause, a higher purpose you are driven to, consumed with? Your cause is a weight you carry like Nehemiah when God called him to rebuild the wall in Jerusalem. Like Nehemiah, your burden only begins to lift as you walk toward your Divine Destiny. What burden or passion are you carrying? Callings are to a person, place, and passion: what ignites your soul into action? What cause (calling) do you have a willingness to suffer for?

2. **STIRRING:** Your MANA will stir you with a Holy Energy in a way other things don't. When in operation, you will feel energized, as if it has unlocked "another person" inside you. This is the Holy Spirit breathing divine power into your inner person. What is hard for others is easy for you: when others are giving up, you are just getting started. You can feel God's design at work

to energize you in your lane. When you feel stirred, pay particular attention to what you feel drawn to do. When Saul was anointed king, the Holy Spirit came upon him, and he "became another man"; His MANA was stirred. The stirring of the Holy Spirit points to your assignment as it did for Saul and Samson as defenders of Israel in their day. *"The child grew up, and the LORD blessed him. And the Spirit of the LORD began to stir him"* (Ref. Judges 13:24-25).

3. **SATISFACTION + JOY:** Your MANA design is linked to your DIVINE DESTINY, so when you are moving within your calling, exercising it, you are satiated in your innermost being. Your MANA at work in your lane of calling satisfies your soul in a way that nothing else can. God's calling on Jeremiah's life was a messenger with a message that had to be delivered. *"But if I say, 'I will not remember Him nor speak anymore in His name, Then in my heart, it becomes like a burning fire shut up in my bones; And I am tired of holding it in, And I cannot endure it'"* (Jeremiah 20:9). God's message was like a fire within him that had to be released. Is there an unmistakable drive, desire, or calling that, when acted upon, satiates your soul? What is the fire in you that needs to be unleashed? Jeremiah was a messenger on a mission. What is your mission?

4. **STUDENT MINDED:** In your MANA, you are a quick study. You pick up things faster than others. Where others struggle, you "just get it." Maybe others have said you're a quick study in a specific something. You are a natural learner in your lane, a 10Xer like Daniel. You seem to have

an intuitive knowledge, a heightened sense of awareness that causes you to capture and comprehend things others don't. Where others see problems, you see solutions like Daniel. Where others see a dead end, you see God's doorway and a path forward. When no one else could solve the problem, it was said of Daniel, *"This was because an extraordinary spirit, knowledge and insight, interpretation of dreams, explanation of riddles, and solving of difficult problems were found in this Daniel, whom the king named Belteshazzar. Let Daniel now be summoned and he will declare the interpretation"* (Daniel 5:12). Daniel received MANA for his assignment in government, but he had to do his part to develop it. Daniel became a student in his lane, diligent in developing and then delivering his MANA for the glory of God. What MANA within you has God chosen to display His glory through?

5. **SINGING IN YOUR SPIRIT:** Your MANA will make your heart sing. Like David swinging his sling, as you run in the lane of your assignment, exercising your gifts, it is as if you have discovered the soundtrack of your spirit. You instinctively know, in your bones, that you are doing what God has made you to do. You are filled with the Spirit as you swing your sling in your marketplace or ministry assignment. One of David's assignments was a songwriter. David wrote over half of the Psalms. As He did, he was filled with the Spirit. David used His gift to play for King Saul, and when he played, the presence of God filled him and Saul and the demons scattered. When moving in your MANA, you will find yourself in your God-given design zone. In it,

you experience God's joy, bliss, and a sense of timelessness as the Holy Spirit moves to work alongside you. It is almost as if you can feel your Creator causing His creation to come alive in you because *it is.* *"So it came about whenever the evil spirit from God came to Saul, David would take the harp and play it with his hand; and Saul would feel relieved and become well, and the evil spirit would leave him"* (1 Samuel 16:23). When you are moving in your design zone, you feel the Holy Spirit awakening within you to come alive alongside you.

6. **SIGNIFICANT SUCCESS:** While moving in your MANA, you may experience early success or an uncommon level of achievement: this is anointed success. Circumstances of life may conspire to catapult you into the limelight or a larger stage whereby your MANA is on display for all to see, like it was when Joseph stood before Pharoah, David before Goliath, or Daniel before the King. God may orchestrate these moments to accelerate you along the path of your Divine Destiny. With your anointed success, God may allow it to spill over to benefit others as it did in the relationship between Joseph and Potiphar. As God was *WITH* Joseph, so He will be with you as you run in your lane of assignment, exercising your MANA for His higher purposes.

> *"And the LORD was with Joseph, so he*
> *became a successful man. And he was in the house of*
> *his master, the Egyptian. Now his master saw that the*
> *LORD was with him and that the LORD made all that*
> *he did prosper in his hand. So Joseph found favor in*
> *his sight and became his personal servant; and he*

7. **SPIRITUAL POWER:** The expression of your MANA is unique to you, a manifestation that sets you apart. It's a divine power that others may recognize before you do. This is the anointing, God's MANA coming alive in you. With your MANA, you can do things others can't. "The women sang as they played and said, 'Saul has slain his thousands, And David his ten thousands'" (1 Samuel 18:7). You are anointed for your assignment. What activities do you do where you hear God more clearly or feel Him working through you? Is there a relative, coach, parent, or boss that has pointed out something you do better than others? In what areas of your life is God touching?

Shortly after my son Casey graduated high school, he was laid up in bed recovering from an ACL surgery. It was a long month in bed, but God used it to open his heart to a few things. Casey realized he needed to change his life and get a new group of friends, and that included leaving his parking attendant job, which kept mixing him up with the wrong crowd. We prayed the prayer of faith over his situation, and God answered quickly. A month later, he was working at a rental car company. Two months after that, his boss quit and Casey told the owner he wanted to take the manager's place. The owner, Eric, replied, "Casey, you are a great employee, and you have a future with our company, but I can't put an 18-year-old in charge of my 200-car rental fleet." A week later, the owner did just that. Within a year, a 19-year-old was now managing an operation with $10 million in rental car inventory, hiring, firing, training, and more. I recognized the hand of God. No one at Casey's age could be put in charge of such a large company and succeed unless God was with him. I witnessed God unlocking Casey's MANA in all seven ways. The 7 Signs of Casey's Spiritual Superpowers came alive all at once. A high school kid who wasn't motivated to get out of bed his senior year a few months earlier was now working 70 hours a week, loving it, and leading at a high level without former training. What was happening? God's MANA was working in Casey. He was learning rapidly, accelerating in success, and clearly was anointed for the assignment in this season of his life. He had found his high calling, his divine destiny. Which of the 7 Signs of a Spiritual Superpower is showing up in your life and in those close to you? As you discover God's MANA within yourself, you will unlock the next piece to walking in your divine destiny.

REFLECT TO CONNECT

1. What is your assignment in this present season?
2. How would you describe the gifts in your MANA Matrix?
3. Assignments are to people, places, and purposes; where do you feel called?

The $100,000 Offer

*"… I count all things to be loss in view of the
surpassing value of knowing Christ Jesus my Lord, for whom I
have suffered the loss of all things,
and count them mere rubbish, so that I may gain Christ"*
Ref. Philippians 3:8.

"At some point, you'll face a moment where you have to decide who lives and who dies." Kevin Costner delivered this powerful line in the movie *The Guardian* to a group of Coast Guard recruits as they watched a ship sinking with people on board. With limited time, energy, and resources, these young Coast Guard swimmers would one day have to make life-altering decisions.

You may not be a first responder, but you, too, will face critical decisions in your walk with Christ. There will come a time when you must choose between the old self and the new self in Christ. Will you follow God's will or your own? Will you choose obedience to Him or pursue your own opportunities?

John Wesley once said, *"I measure all things by the price they will pay in eternity."* Early in my walk with Christ, I often chose my own way over God's. I always had a good reason, but as I grew older, those reasons faded. Now, I make major life decisions by putting them in God's hands first. Have you ever had to choose Christ over a paycheck, a promotion, or peer pressure? How did you handle it?

Have you ever wrestled with a decision that could make or lose you a lot of money? I have been in my industry for a long time, and at one point, I was restless and ready for a change. While on vacation, my son Bailey met a new friend at the hotel pool. We met the parents, and it turned out we were in the same industry, and so we hit it off quickly. Long after our vacation, I stayed in touch with David, the dad. After some time, David asked me if I'd consider coming to work for him. Before he could make me an offer, I told him it would have to be $100,000 more than I was currently making. It was my way of throwing up a trial balloon to scare him off. I knew he could not offer me that much, so I felt there was little risk of having to make a big decision. I was wrong. He offered me $100,000 more than I was making. Now, I was in trouble. I committed to a decision but had not run it by God first. I reasoned within myself, "This must be the hand of God and an answer to my prayer about how to pay for my kids' education." Have you ever justified something you wanted before taking it to God for His input?

WILL I CHOOSE MY PERSONAL PROSPERITY OVER GOD'S PURPOSES?

*"It's comforting to know that all my life decisions
go through God's hands first."*
~Scott Hogle

Have you ever gone into prayer with your mind made up? I have done this more times than I can count! How about you? Proverbs 3:5 instructs us to *"Lean not unto our own understanding, but in all our ways to acknowledge him, and he* *will direct our paths."* I showed up in prayer the next day with my mind already made up. When I asked God what I should do about the job offer, the heavens were silent; there was no answer. After weeks of frustration, I asked my pastor's advice. He did not tell me what to do, but he did pray for me. As he did, I heard God whisper to me, "Step slowly away from that door." It was a time in my life when my soul felt lean, and a job prospect along with the promotion and pay raise was exciting. I was ready for advancement and change. But God said no. The way He said no suggested that I was now at risk. His direction to <u>step slowly away</u> said everything. I wrestled with this for a few days and then called David to tell him I wouldn't be taking the job. With the door now closed, I spent a month in depression, wrestling with my decision. Have you ever wrestled with the Word of the Lord when He said no to something you wanted?

ACCEPTING OF THE ASSIGNMENT

"Your marketplace vocation is your ministry unto the Lord, let this sink into your spirit." ~Scott Hogle

That night, I talked to my wife about what God had said, and she suggested that maybe God has me in my current place of employment for a good reason. She asked, "What if God wanted you there another ten years? Would you stay?"

I was so frustrated with that idea I lashed out and yelled, "Don't say that; I don't want to hear it," and headed down to my home office to be alone.

As I leaned back in my chair, the Lord said, "You have prayed to me for some of the souls in your office. What if it took another ten years? Would you stay then?"

"Well, of course I would Lord; what's ten years in eternity?" That night, I went to bed and cried myself to sleep. I had surrendered and resigned myself to the fact that a long season of unhappiness was ahead of me. Although I said "yes" and knew I was being obedient, it did not feel good. This is often the case initially. A short time later, I found the determination and strength in my spirit, and I said to God, "Alright then, let's get to work on what You want me to do here so I can move on." Then, the strangest thing started to happen. People I worked with, clients I had lunch with, and people out of the blue began to engage me in God conversations. Some were saved, some delivered, and others were prayed for. While I passed on the pay and promotion, God opened the door to a higher purpose. When I gave up the temporal for the eternal, God opened new doors of fruitfulness in the ministry and the marketplace.

There will be times in your life when you must choose between yourself and God, between the temporal and the eternal. You may not be serving in the Coast Guard, but you are in the business of saving lives and prioritizing God's eternal purposes over temporary prosperity. Don't be surprised if sacrificing temporal blessings turns out to be a test, and God brings those blessings back around. Every successful test comes with a passing grade, and with each passing grade comes a promotion, whether in the spiritual realm, the natural world, or sometimes both.

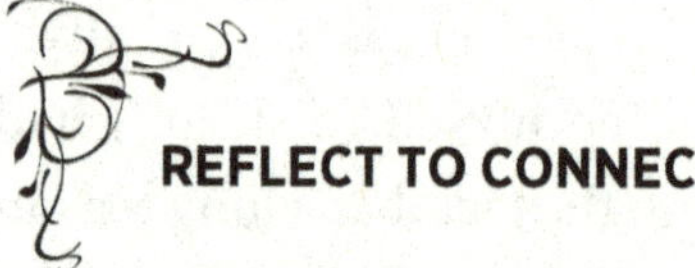

REFLECT TO CONNECT

1. When was the last time you wrestled with something God asked you to do?
2. What happened when you prioritized your will over God's? What was the outcome?
3. Is God prompting you in any way to shift your priorities? If so, how?

The Boaz Blessing

"And Ruth the Moabitess said to Naomi, 'Please let me go to the field and glean among the ears of grain following one in whose eyes I may find favor.' And Naomi said to her, 'Go, my daughter.' So Ruth left and went and gleaned in the field after the reapers; <u>and she happened</u> to come to the portion of the field belonging to Boaz" Ruth 2:2-3.

When God wants to bless you, He will bring you a **Boaz!** Naomi, while living in Moab, lost her husband and two sons and journeyed back to Bethlehem with her daughter-in-law, Ruth. A famine in the land drove Naomi and her family from Bethlehem, and now different types of "famine" would drive these two women back to Bethlehem. Famines come in many forms. There are famines of love where you may be experiencing a season of loneliness. There are famines of finances, barrenness, joblessness, and more. If you are experiencing leanness in your soul, you could be experiencing a famine of purpose and need God to open a door of opportunity. We all experience famines—famines of favor, provision, love, and more. Ruth and Naomi arrived in Bethlehem alone, poor, and with few options to support themselves. Little did they know that their lives were about to change—God was about to send them a Boaz.

In Israel, there was a Law of Gleaning that allowed the poor to follow behind harvesters and collect leftover crops so they would have food to eat. Ruth stepped up and offered to glean, a humbling task. As she entered the field to glean, she found herself in the field of a man named Boaz, who would take great interest in her. Through her relationship with Boaz, God would turn her famines into fruitfulness. Everything God does happens through a person or place. If you are praying and waiting in expectation for an answered prayer, be on the lookout for a Boaz. Whenever God wants to bring a blessing into your life, He will send a Boaz! There are dozens of characteristics of a Boaz Blessing; how many can you identify? Here are a few ways in which God uses a Boaz to usher in a season of blessing.

CHARACTERISTICS OF A BOAZ

"Mark those who are doubly good to you; it's a sign God has paired you with them to move you and His purposes forward." ~Scott Hogle

A Boaz works with God's hand of providential positioning. Ruth HAPPENED to show up in Boaz's field. It was not a coincidence but God's hand of providence guiding Ruth. God can bring you to the right people, at the right time, in the right place, and under the right circumstances. It may not feel like God is at work or that nothing is happening behind the scenes, but there is, and it is God's hand directing your steps. God does not cause famine in our lives, but that does not mean he won't use them to get us moving. God would use famine to position Naomi in Moab but then use famine again to reposition Naomi and Ruth back in Bethlehem. If you are experiencing a "famine" in your life, consider asking God where He wants you to go and WHO he wants you to see.

During a season of joblessness, I found myself in a lengthy interview cycle for a general sales manager position at five radio stations in Hawaii. I was doing well, and after two months of interviewing, I entered the third round. Suddenly, the person who was interviewing me left the company. I received a call from the new interviewer who was taking over. I was exhausted and frustrated that I had to start over. But it turned out the person interviewing me knew one of the people I used as a reference! He had worked with him previously and greatly respected him. As it was with Ruth, when she HAPPENED to show up in Boaz's field, my new interviewer HAPPENED to work with someone I had listed as a reference. God would use my work famine to position me with a new supervisor who would become a mentor and friend for many years. What I saw as a delay, God was using as a doorway.

A Boaz is a door-opener who provides uncommon favor. Boaz showed incredible kindness to Ruth, and the scripture points out that Boaz NOTICED HER and showed her favor. A Boaz in your life will notice you and take a special interest in you. Where others saw Ruth as a foreigner, Boaz saw her as special. Where others see disadvantages, a Boaz in your life will see uniqueness. Where some may see weakness, others will see God's strength in you. Where others may be repelled or disinterested in you, a Boaz will be attracted and drawn to you. A Boaz will show you uncommon favor, which can show up as doors of opportunity or mentorship or simply by connecting you with the right people, which will pave the way to a brighter future. After graduating high school, my wife Kate auditioned at the University of Hawaii for a scholarship in dance and drama. While there, someone NOTICED something special about her and encouraged her to come back the following week. The following week, a team from USC visited and they NOTICED something special in her and offered her a scholarship. Her trajectory would change, and she would find herself on the way to one of the greatest schools in the country. How did this happen? God sent a Boaz to notice her and show her uncommon favor.

A Boaz is one who honors you by seeing and then speaking to the best in you. Boaz knew of Ruth's story and how faithful she had been to her mother-in-law Naomi. Ruth had a reputation for being better to her mother-in-law than seven sons were to their mothers. *"For your daughter-in-law, who loves you and who is better to you than seven sons"* (Ruth 4:15). Scripture also uses the word "Noble" to describe Ruth. While others saw a foreigner with a past that didn't fit in, Boaz saw nobility in Ruth. When God brings a Boaz into your life, that person will talk to you like Boaz talked to Ruth, with great respect and honor. Who do you know who sees more in you than others, who is always encouraging and uplifting you? These are the Boaz's God has positioned on your path; stay close to them. They are operating under the shadow of the Almighty to show you favor. I have been fortunate to find a Boaz in every season of life. *Mark those who are doubly good to you*; it's a sign God has paired you with them to move you and His purposes forward.

A Boaz is one who protects and provides. Boaz didn't just like Ruth; he LOOKED OUT for her and made sure she had an EXTRA return from her labor. He never sent her home to Naomi empty-handed. A Boaz will show you the lay of the land to help you get ahead. They will use their influence to direct you and others to make sure you are taken care of, even protected. A Boaz puts their arm of influence around you so others know you are "with them.'" When others looked down on Timothy, a young and inexperienced preacher in Ephesus, The Apostle Paul made sure people knew he approved of him. Is there someone you can extend your influence to? Is there a Boaz God is leading you to get close to? Who can you provide for or protect in your church, community, or job? When God wants to bless you, He will send you a Boaz!

REFLECT TO CONNECT

1. Who can you be a Boaz to?
2. Who have been the Boazs in your life?
3. What is the evidence of the Boazs in your life?

Generational Assignments

"For I have chosen him, so that he may command his children and his household after him to keep the way of the LORD by doing righteousness and justice, so that the LORD may bring upon Abraham what He has spoken about him"
Genesis 18:19.

There is a transfer of anointing and assignment that can happen between people. This transfer happened between Jesus and the twelve disciples, Paul and Timothy, Elijah and Elisha, Saul and David, and so on. In Abraham's day, there was a generational assignment that transferred within their family. Blessing, favor, and fruitfulness flowed to Issac, then to Jacob, and so on. Each played their role as God's greater purposes unfolded throughout the generations. God gave His WHY for choosing Abraham when He pointed out that Abraham would teach his children the Ways of the Lord. A responsibility that comes with carrying the mantle of the Lord. The anointing rests upon both the assignment and the person stewarding it. If the responsibility of the assignment is not stewarded well, the anointing or assignment can be forfeited as it was with Esau, King Saul, and Samson.

Assignments and blessings can be forfeited. Esau forfeited his birthright. In Issac's day, there was a transfer of assignment, favor, and authority from Esau to Jacob because God was displeased with Esau for thinking so lowly of the inheritance and blessing that went to the first son. The relative who was first in line to marry Ruth chose his prosperity over duty and forfeited an incredible inheritance to be in the lineage of Jesus. Boaz stepped up to take his place. Ruth and Boaz then gave birth to Obed, who bore Jesse, who bore David, and on to the lineage of Jesus. When one person steps down, another steps up to take the assignment in the Kingdom of God. King Saul disqualified himself as God's chosen man when he chose sacrifice over obedience, and then David took his place. God takes kingdom assignments and duty seriously and expects us to steward the mantle of anointing that comes with them. What has God given you to steward?

> "When one person steps down, another steps up to take the assignment in the Kingdom of God." ~Scott Hogle

What has been given to you? My grandfather Paul asked me the same question, over and over, whenever I would go to visit him. I was in my 20s, sitting with Grandpa Paul, and he asked me about my life. When I would speak of someone, his first question, as always, was, "Do they have the Christ?" The conversation continued and when someone else came up, Grandpa Paul asked me again, "Do they have the Christ?" My grandfather's passion for keeping the Gospel a priority in relationships was very evident. In my younger years, that question didn't mean as much to me as it does today. Little did I know that God was transferring an assignment that would birth a new anointing in me down the road. Today, I have a God-given burden for the people I work with, those I preach to on the weekends, and those I converse with. As a younger man, my grandfather had a burden to preach but couldn't because he only had an eighth-grade education; he wasn't allowed in his day. Yet God would give him an anointing to write hymns that are still being sung in Ukrainian churches around the world today. God gave him the assignment and anointing for singing and writing music, and I was given the assignment of speaking, teaching, and preaching the Good News. Is there an assignment you have received generationally or through proximity to a dedicated man or woman of God?

DIVINE ASSIGNMENTS PASS THROUGH THE GENERATIONS

"To take hold of the assignment and anointing God is imparting to you, you may need to let go of one thing so you can grab hold of the God thing." ~Scott Hogle

Do you remember the place, date, and circumstances surrounding your assignment? I was driving into my parking garage many years after my grandfather had passed, and his recurring question came to mind, "Do they have the Christ?" As this memory resurfaced, I was suddenly overcome by the Holy Spirit. An impartation was taking place, and I began to weep. I wasn't sad or happy; it was God's way of saying, "I'm giving this to you now, and I want you to know where it came from." There was a transfer taking place.

Transfers of assignments and anointings and the impartation of spiritual giftings can take place in a family but also through prayer and the ministry of "laying on of hands" (Hebrews 6:2). If you were to ask my grandfather about the moment of assignment and anointing in his life, he would point to an act of obedience that unlocked his anointing and led to worldwide fruitfulness in his music. Before knowing the Lord, he sang and played instruments. Years later, after he had come to know the Lord, a pastor asked him to move his family to another state to serve as choir director. Grandpa Paul didn't want to go, and he resisted the idea. He even performed a "Gideon fleece." A Gideon fleece is when you ask God to confirm his call with a sign. God answered and confirmed the call to accept this assignment, but he still hesitated.

One afternoon, while napping, the front door blew open, and he heard God's voice in the wind saying, "Paul, you have to go." At that moment, he chose to obey. To take hold of the assignment and anointing God is imparting to you, you may need to let go of one thing so you can grab hold of the God thing. To grab hold of the assignment and anointing God had for my grandfather, he had to let go of something else—a good job and a home he had built with his own hands.

What is God asking you to release? Is there a divine conversation He's been having with you? One step of obedience can unlock your future and set you back on the path toward your Divine Destiny. What is God laying on your heart right now?

DIVINE CONVERSATIONS UNLOCK THE WHAT, WHO, AND WHERE GOD IS CALLING YOU

"There is a transfer, an exchange, a depositing of Divine Destiny that can come upon you when you are in proximity of those carrying an anointing and assignment. The impartation can happen as you hear their 'God Story.'" ~Scott Hogle

What is the intersection of your origin story and assignment? I once asked God to show me where my Grandfather Paul may have received an assignment or anointing. The memory that came to me was of him visiting a man named John Barchuk in Chicago, Illinois. He and John Barchuk met in the German work camps during WWII. John would become a preacher, author, and primary figure in the Ukrainian Baptist Church in the U.S. after the war ended. Some have referred to him as the "Billy Graham"' of the Ukrainian God movement in the U.S. My grandfather stayed with John for a few months in his 30s while looking for work before moving his family from Sandstone, MN, to Chicago, Illinois. Night after night, they would speak of the Lord at the dinner table. It is said that "character transfers face to face." During those conversations, God's heart, flowing through John, imprinted on my grandfather's heart. In that transfer, a supernatural impartation of God's heart took place, making God's priorities, my grandfather's priorities, and God's desires his desires. There is a transfer, an exchange, a depositing of assignments, and an anointing that can come upon you when you are in proximity to those carrying an anointing and assignment. This transfer happens in conversations, face-to-face and even in the laying on of hands. Sometimes, it is within your family line; other times, it will be from someone God puts you in proximity to. Being willing to share your story with friends, your kids, and grandkids is God's design to impart the anointing and assignment. Sometimes, it comes in the form of a question from a grandparent to a grandchild. Is there someone you can ask about their "God story" to see if God will unlock your story as you hear theirs?

Is there someone you can share your God story with? Here are a few conversation starters I use to share my story while I wait for God to open a door of interest in them. I use these to open doors of conversation because I believe that as I initiate a God-directed conversation and they hear my story, God will talk to them about their story and an impartation will take place, moving them ever closer to their Divine Destiny. You can do the same.

REFLECT TO CONNECT

1. There is something I am struggling with. May I share it with you and ask you to speak to it? (When you are vulnerable first, it gives others permission to open up, too.)
2. I had an experience with God; may I share it with you? (Asking permission to get personal with someone can pave the way for intimate conversation.)
3. Your opinion means a lot to me. Would you be willing to help me process something out loud? (Talk it out to draw it out.)

The Shield of Favor

*"For You bless the righteous person, LORD,
You surround him with favor as with a shield"* Psalm 5:12.

God's Favor is an invisible power that flows through you and influences those around you visibly. With God's Favor, you walk into a room, and the room is charged with an attitude of acceptance toward you. Favor predisposes people to serve you and say yes to you. Favor goes before you to speak to those in your world to move them to bless you, open doors for you, and become a way-maker for you. God's shield of Favor has benefits beyond blessing; it can protect you from attacks, both natural and spiritual. God said to Abraham in Genesis 15:1, "I am your shield." This means that when natural or spiritual enemies come at you, God's Favor forces them to bless you and not hurt you. A king named Balik tried to hire a prophet named Balaam to curse Israel. But Balaam could not because God's shield of Favor surrounded Israel. In the same way, when you accepted Christ, you became a child of God and came under his protection.

PRAYING FOR FAVOR

"Favor can do in a day what hard work can't do in a decade."
~Scott Hogle

You need God's Favor to reach your Divine Destiny! A shield is a crucial part of a soldier's armor. Without it, the soldier is unprotected, and its benefits remain unused. Similarly, God's shield of Favor must be brought into your daily life. This Divine Favor can lie dormant and unused if not actively sought, asked for, and cooperated with. It must be acknowledged and engaged daily to experience God's Favor fully.

As a young man striving to get ahead professionally, I would often ask God, "Lord, please grant me favor with God and man." If I had a meeting coming up with a client, I would ask God to give me insight for the meeting and Favor with the client. If I had an evaluation with a supervisor, I would ask God for Favor. If I speak to a large group and need to persuade an audience, I ask God for Favor. Knowing I am praying in accordance with His Will, He grants my request. God wants to do the same for you when you start seeking His Favor for the situations you face. God's *Favor can do more for you in a day than what hard work can achieve in a decade.* Favor can open doors that were shut. Favor can cause someone to like you who doesn't even know you. Favor is the invisible charisma of Christ that flows through you to draw people toward you. Favor is God speaking to others on your behalf. Favor can move you to the front of the line, soften a person's heart toward you, or put you in a position for that raise and promotion you've been working for. God's Favor can melt a hardened heart, turn a situation around, and set your feet on a firm foundation. Favor is the invisible force of God working on your behalf to move you along the path of your Divine Destiny.

*"Once you taste God's flow of Favor in your life,
you'll never want to leave its current."* ~Scott Hogle

In my bestselling devotional *Divine Intelligence,* I write about the secret and supernatural positioning of a man named Mordecai. God wanted to position Mordecai in the king's court so he could play a key role in saving Israel. How did the king learn about Mordecai, whom he had never met? God caused the king to have a sleepless night, and when he awoke, he asked for the chronicles of the king to be read to him. As they were read, he discovered a story about an informant who had informed the court of a secret plot to kill the king. That informant was Mordecai, who stepped out and risked himself to save the king—that sleepless night led to Mordecai's promotion into the king's court and a position of power. While the book of Esther tells the story of Esther and how she saved Israel, the book of Esther ends with Mordechai being in a position to administer God's will in Persia. God knows how to move those in authority so you are positioned and promoted to administrate His will. Favor is given for God's purposes, not solely for our personal benefit.

THE PATH TO FAVOR

Problem-solving in the place you are called is God's primary way to create Favor. One of the ways God creates Favor is to allow a problem to emerge "in the natural" that only He can solve in the supernatural. For 40 days, Goliath stood in front of the armies of Israel, taunting them. It created fear and embarrassment for the army of Israel but an opportunity for David. The stage was now set for a demonstration in front of the entire nation, to showcase the anointing of God upon David's life. Acting with courage and the supernatural speed and accuracy of his sling, David moved in the supernatural anointing to solve a problem that Israel and King Saul could not. In a similar situation, Pharaoh had a dream no one could interpret except a slave named Joseph. After interpreting the dream and solving a crisis for Pharaoh, Joseph was promoted to the second most powerful position in the land. God's supernatural gift of Favor can flow through you to solve problems in your marketplace and ministry assignments. God does this to advance his purposes and move his agenda forward while at the same time establishing you in the lane He has called you. God's Favor will position, promote, and set you apart for the work ahead, as it did with Joseph, Daniel, Mordecai, Esther, David, and the saints who have gone before you. Favor is a critical tool for your assignment and a powerful weapon God uses to advance you and His purposes.

> *"Then Pharaoh said to his servants, 'Can we find a man like this, in whom there is a divine spirit?' So Pharaoh said to Joseph, 'Since God has informed you of all this, there is no one as discerning and wise as you are. You shall be in charge of my house, and all my people shall be obedient to you; only regarding the throne will I be greater than you.'"* Genesis 41:38-40

THE FLOW OF FAVOR COMES WITH RESPONSIBILITY

Become a student of Favor. All the supernatural Favor in the world will not help you if you do not do your part. Joseph, Daniel, and David excelled where God placed them, allowing God to work through them. If Mordecai had been incompetent in his new role, how long do you think he would have kept his job? God is willing and able to do his part, but there is a part that He expects from you. There is always a part you will play in the natural to usher in the supernatural in the lanes of calling you find yourself. This includes showing up early and staying late, becoming a student in your lane, striving for continual improvement and excellence, involving God in your daily doings, and submitting your ways to Him so He can direct you. As you do your part to create natural success, it allows God to open the door for supernatural Favor to flow through you. *Once you taste God's flow of Favor, you'll never want to leave its current.* You will walk through your days with His Shield of Favor.

REFLECT TO CONNECT

1. In what situations do you need God's Favor?
2. Is there an impossible problem no one can solve that you can bring to God?
3. What practical steps can you take to create Favor with a loved one, a supervisor, or someone with whom you desire to get close?

God Winks & Windshield Worship

"But thou art holy, O thou that inhabitest the praises of Israel" Psalm 22:3 (KJV).

God doesn't just inhabit the praise of His people; when you worship Him, He fills you with His presence. Ever since I can remember, my wife Kate has always named our cars. When she had a black Honda van, she called it the Black Pearl, after the ship in *Pirates of the Caribbean*. Her white BMW is Elsa, named after the character in the movie *Frozen*. There is a car we used to take on long road trips across the country, and she called it the Roadrunner. I grew up road-tripping across the Midwest with my family; you could say I like long journeys in the car. I enjoy the long stretches of solitude, thinking, and listening to audiobooks and worship music. Long stretches of uninterrupted "me time" allow me to decompress, get quiet before God, and enjoy extended worship and downtime. In today's fast-paced lifestyle, taking time to separate from the fast pace of life and lean hard into the presence of God is non-negotiable for me. Extended solitude restores my bandwidth. Cars have always had a seasonal symbolism in my life, almost as if they signaled a transition from one season to the next. Maybe you've heard of this scripture, *"To every car and commute under heaven, there is a purpose and season."* That's from the book of "Scott."

How do you create an atmosphere of praise in your life? It's all about being intentional with what I allow into my environment. By carefully choosing what I allow in and keep out, I pave the way for the anointing to flow freely and consistently in my life. My new vehicle is like a worship wagon, a vault of silence I can shut myself into, just me and God. The day we picked up my new Honda Ridgeline, it came pre-programmed with four Christian Radio stations. To this day, we don't know how that happened. And can you guess what happened next? Yes, my new ride got a new name. It was named the Worship Wagon by you know who. I often use my commute time for worship time. Worship is a sure-fire way to attract the presence of God. God doesn't just inhabit the praise of his people; He inhabits YOU when you worship Him. While we worship, God is busy making a way where there seems to be no way. It is in worship that seasons change, bondages are broken, favor is unlocked, healing takes place, and what you've been praying for is loosed, released, and granted. Some of my most incredible ideas, insights, and breakthroughs have come to me while worshiping and praying in the spirit while I drive. Some people have eureka moments in the shower; I get mine behind the wheel. For this reason, I always keep a notepad and pen in my car.

DRIVE TIME IS NOW PRAYER TIME

"He who dwells in the secret place of the Most High,
Shall abide under the shadow of the Almighty." Psalm 91:1

Consider sanctifying your commute. When our kids were young, we redeemed the drive time to school by praying with them. I always had them recite the Lord's Prayer with me. On the other hand, Kate taught them to put on the Armor of God when she took them to school. We affectionately termed our time with God in the car as Windshield Worship. In those moments, no matter how short the drive, it gave us great comfort knowing we covered our kids with a blanket of prayer and worship before they went off to school. Sanctifying your drive time into God-time sets the tone for the rest of your day. Prayer and worship on the drive create a sort of spiritual halo effect you get to carry with you throughout your day.

DRIVE TIME INTERRUPTED

*"It is not God who leaves our presence, but we who leave
His. If you cannot find God, go back to the last place you left
Him, and there you will find Him waiting for you."*
~Scott Hogle

During one of my wintertime road trips, driving late at night on I15 in Utah, I passed a person walking on the side of the road. I was doing about 80 MPH on a cold February night, and it struck me that this person didn't have a coat. I looked down at my instrument panel, and it was 32 degrees outside. My first thought was, "What in the world is this person doing walking outside in the middle of the night without a coat?" I had been driving all day, had a hotel stop in mind a couple of hours up the road, and was rushing to reach my destination. A nagging feeling told me I should stop and pick this person up, but I shrugged it off because I was tired. I was on a mission to get to my hotel, but God had another mission in mind. God said to me, "If it were your son, you'd want someone to stop." I did what most Christians do—I asked myself, "Is this you God?" I knew the Lord's voice, and even through my tiredness, I couldn't deny His interruption in my drive and His intervention in this person's life. I had to drive another ten miles before seeing the exit sign that allowed me to swing around and pick up this late-night walker. I caught up to him, and as I got closer, I thought, "This person must be stupid; they are out in the middle of nowhere in 32-degree weather. They are going to freeze to death." I pulled alongside him and offered a ride. He turned out to be a high school teenage boy. He said he was meeting his brother at a Walmart thirty miles up the road. I don't know if that was the truth, but I persisted in the conversation and sensed he might not have a place to stay the night. When we reached his exit, I suggested I drop him at Motel 6 and buy him a night stay. He accepted, and I gave him $100 to pay for the room. I also gave him a jacket I strangely bought the day before at Kohl's but didn't know why. Now I knew. I felt compelled to buy that jacket even though I did not need one.

Some people call this a God Wink. A God Wink is when God's serendipity shows up on your path and suddenly you know why. God makes two things happen: you are involved, and He connects the dots for you. I also gave the young man a copy of my book *Persuade* since it was next to the jacket in my trunk. I then prayed for him before we parted ways. I don't know what happened to him, but I helped to the degree he let me, and I did what God prompted me to do. It was a Good Samaritan moment, and God chose me to be that Good Samaritan. God may drop a whisper in your heart during your windshield worship that has nothing to do with you. When people pray, God sends someone to answer that prayer; that's how it works. If you consider how your prayers get answered, it always happens through a person and place. If that young man prayed for a jacket that night, I was the person God sent to provide it. Who might God be sending you to help today? You are an answer to someone's prayer; God wants to wink at you.

GOD WINKS & WINDSHIELD WHISPERS

"The more you chase God, the more He will be found by you."
~Scott Hogle

Because I seek God while in my car, it is there God often speaks to me. Sitting in a parking garage at Ala Moana Mall in Honolulu, Hawaii, I asked God when he was going to do something to help me launch into a new season; I was tired of waiting. He replied, "I'm waiting for you." Sitting in a parking garage at the doctor's office, looking at a medical report with words I couldn't understand, God asked me, "Whose report are you going to believe?" I answered, "Yours, of course, Lord." God can speak to you anywhere; where do you hear Him best? When God speaks to me in the car, sometimes His word to me is not something I want to hear, yet it's necessary for that season.

God's whispers and winks in your life are essential to you fulfilling your Divine Destiny. Knowing God's word and his principles will only get you so far. Eventually, you'll need to rely on a "word spoken in due season" to navigate life's challenges. It is during Windshield Worship time that I redeem the micro-moments in my day so I can intersect with the Divine. I press in and pursue the Holy to apprehend He who desires to apprehend me. The more you chase after God, the more He will be found by you. He desires your presence more than you desire His. If you're struggling to want more of God, pray this simple prayer, "Dear Lord, please give me a heart after yours, and make your desires my desires." This simple prayer will give you a heart to worship. Before long, you'll start receiving God Winks during your Windshield Worship time.

"Your ears will hear a word behind you, saying, 'This is the way, walk in it,' whenever you turn to the right or to the left."
Isaiah 30:21

REFLECT TO CONNECT

1. In what ways can you redeem the micro-moments in your day to repurpose them into worship?
2. If the dashboard in your car was the dashboard for your life, what would the gauges read?
3. What is your last instruction, inspiring thought, or contact point with God?

Becoming an Abigail

"But Nabal answered David's servants and said, 'Who is David? And who is the son of Jesse? There are many servants today who are each breaking away from his master. Shall I then take my bread and my water and my meat that I have slaughtered for my shearers, and give it to men whose origin I do not know?' So David's young men retraced their way and went back; and they came and told him according to all these words. David said to his men, 'Each of you gird on his sword.' So each man girded on his sword. And David also girded on his sword, and about four hundred men went up behind David while two hundred stayed with the baggage" 1 Samuel 25:10-13.

David and his mighty men protected Nabal's fields, property, and shepherds from threats in the wilderness. When David asked for a little consideration in return (some food for his men), Nabal didn't just say "no"; he insulted David's kindness and dealt harshly with him. Nabal was returning evil for good, sending David into a rage. David determined to kill Nabal for the offense. It's the only time in scripture that we see David fall into anger and lose control. But Abigail, Nabal's wife, moves quickly to intercept David and smooth over the offense.

"David said to Abigail, 'Praise be to the LORD, the God of Israel, who has sent you today to meet me. May you be blessed for your good judgment and for keeping me from bloodshed this day and from avenging myself with my own

hands. Otherwise, as surely as the LORD, *the God of Israel,
lives, who has kept me from harming you, if you had not come
quickly to meet me, not one male belonging to Nabal would
have been left alive by daybreak.'"* 1 Samuel 32-34

At great personal risk, she courageously faced danger to save her husband and her people. Abigail's wise actions and eloquent words created an atmosphere of honor, humility, and respect in her interactions with David. David is so impressed with Abigail's way of communicating that he not only follows her advice but later marries her. Abigail shows herself to be a woman of wisdom, grace, and honor. How did she do it? How can you become an Abigail? Here is how the scenario played out.

7 QUALITIES TO BECOMING AN ABIGAIL

1. ABIGAILS ACT WITH DISCERNMENT + SPEED: Did you know there is a skill for handling difficult A-type personalities? After hearing of the trouble Nabal created with David, Abigail <u>acts quickly</u> to send a messenger to thank and recognize David for the kindness he and his men had shown in protecting Nabal's property and staff in the fields. Why did she do this? To buy time while she prepared a gift for David. It is almost as if Abigail has been here before, having to cover for her husband's offenses. Do you have someone you often find yourself covering for or making excuses for? Abigail's decision to send a messenger with the announcement of an upcoming gift reflects her understanding of Biblical wisdom found in Proverbs 18:16,

"A person's gift makes room for them and brings them before great people." Expressing gratitude through a gift demonstrates appreciation, respect, and honor. Gracious words with a gift have a way of displacing the emotion surrounding the issue at hand. Just as Jacob sent gifts ahead of him to reconcile with Esau, we see the power of giving in making peace. When you approach God with thanksgiving and enter His courts with praise, as encouraged in Psalm 100:4, He welcomes you in.

2. ABIGAILS KNOW HOW TO HANDLE PEOPLE OF POWER AND EGO: Are you willing to humble yourself even when you feel you are right to keep the peace or calm someone down? "When Abigail saw David, she hurried and dismounted from her donkey and bowed herself to the ground. She fell at his feet and said, 'On me alone, my lord, be the blame. And please let your maidservant speak to you, and listen to the words of your maidservant.'" Abigail was quick to humble herself and take responsibility for something her husband did. David saw her standing in the gap for his offense. She then asks permission to speak to David. It captured David's attention. Abigail's mission was reconciliation, regardless of who committed the offense. She prioritized reconciliation above being right and took responsibility for something that wasn't her fault. In my home, I am the chief officer in charge of reconciliation. That means I repent first. I humble myself first. I am the first to take the high road. Is it easy? Absolutely not! However, modeling reconciliation shows my family that I

put Christ above my ego. Isn't it better to be wrong and reconciled than right and separated? If I have committed an offense or I am in a situation where someone is upset or angry, I go into "question mode" because questions are inviting. I will ask questions like the following:

- Would you be willing to forgive me?
- What can I do that will make things right?
- May I ask your permission to speak to you about a difficult situation?
- I know I don't have the right to ask, but would you be willing to hear me out?
- Can you help me understand where you are coming from? I want to understand your side.

3. ABIGAILS SHOW PEOPLE GOD'S HAND WORKING IN THEIR LIFE: Do you speak to people about God's hand in their lives? Abigail then said, *"Now therefore, my lord, as the LORD lives, and as your soul lives, <u>since the LORD has restrained you</u> from shedding blood, and from avenging yourself by your own hand, now then let your enemies and those who seek evil against my lord, be as Nabal."* Abigail knew of David's closeness with God, so she invoked the higher authority in her conversation. She was on the right side of right, and when David heard it, he heard God's voice in her words.

4. ABIGAILS TALK TO PEOPLE ABOUT GOD'S FUTURE FOR THEM: Abigail goes on to say, *"Please forgive the transgression of your maidservant; for the*

LORD will certainly make for my lord an enduring house, because my lord is fighting the battles of the LORD, and evil will not be found in you all your days." Abigail's poise and skill remind David of the <u>bigger picture</u>, his assignment, and the importance of remaining innocent before the Lord. How did she do this? By painting a picture in David's mind that reminded him of God's future for him. Is there someone you can talk to about their future and the God potential you see in them? It's rare that someone talks to us about our potential and God's best for our lives, but when it happens, it unlocks a God-level conversation. Who can you be an Abigail to today?

5. ABIGAILS DRAW OUT THE BEST BY SPEAKING TO THE BEST IN PEOPLE: Abigail isn't just stroking David's ego when she speaks to him about his gift and the moment of greatness everyone witnessed when he killed Goliath with a sling. She said, *"Should anyone rise up to pursue you and to seek your life, then the life of my lord shall be bound in the bundle of the living with the LORD your God; but the lives of your enemies He will sling out as from the hollow of a sling."* Abigail speaks to David about his gift and acknowledges how that gift in operation catapulted him to national stardom when he used it to kill Goliath. We all need to be reminded by others about the gifts and greatness God has given us. As Abigail speaks to David about his sling, his heart is enlarged and edified by the honor she is showing him. Her words to David about his giftedness also point out that she is observant and can speak to

him about his greatness. Is there someone you can have a conversation with about the gifts and greatness God has put in them?

6. ABIGAILS REMIND PEOPLE ABOUT THE GREAT THINGS AHEAD FOR THEM: Abigail goes on to say, *"And when the LORD does for my lord according to all the good that He has spoken concerning you, and appoints you ruler over Israel."* Very few people speak to us about us. Kids need parents to provide a vision of what can be; this gives them hope. We all need leaders to help us see who and what we can become and what we can attain. Is there someone you can have a conversation with about their potential? I am intentional about doing this with my employees, wife, and kids. Having a meaningful conversation with someone about their future can unlock possibilities and reveal God's open door of Divine Destiny for them.

7. ABIGAILS BOLDLY SPEAK UP FOR THEMSELVES: Abigail is about to insert herself into David's future by courageously asking David not to forget about her. She says, *"...this will not cause grief or a troubled heart to my lord, both by having shed blood without cause and by my lord having avenged himself. When the LORD deals well with my lord, then remember your maidservant."* Abigail successfully switch-pitched David from his course of action while at the same time endearing herself to him.

Then David said to Abigail, *"Blessed be the LORD God of Israel, who sent you this day to meet me, and blessed be your discernment, and blessed be you, who have kept me this day from bloodshed and from avenging myself by my own hand.*" David acknowledged Abigail's words and actions <u>as inspired by the Lord</u>. David praises Abigail for her wisdom, honor, and grace. *"So David received from her hand what she had brought him and said to her, 'Go up to your house in peace. See, I have listened to you and granted your request.'"* Abigail demonstrated the graciousness and wisdom of God, and David recognized them. When she became a widow, he wed her. *How she spoke made her memorable.*

REFLECT TO CONNECT

1. In what ways can you practice the honor, grace, humility, and wisdom of Abigail?
2. Do you know someone who has to work overtime managing a relationship like Abigail did with Nabal?
3. Who do you know who is as skillful as Abigail when dealing with forceful and powerful men like Nabal and David?

Spiritual Spidey Senses

"They went to Joshua to the camp at Gilgal and said to him and to the men of Israel, 'We have come from a far country; now therefore, make a covenant with us.' The men of Israel said to the Hivites, 'Perhaps you are living within our land; how then shall we make a covenant with you?' So the men of Israel took some of their provisions, <u>and did not ask for the counsel of the LORD</u>. Joshua made peace with them and made a covenant with them, to let them live; and the leaders of the congregation swore an oath to them"

Joshua 9:6-7, 14.

Have you ever been on the cusp of making a decision, then paused because you knew something wasn't quite right? God may give you a "check" in your heart as a heads-up when something is being hidden from you. God did this for Israel by giving them a check in their spirit, but they ignored it. Have you ever felt a check in your spirit but proceeded anyway? Israel questioned the Gibeonite's story but ignored God's prompting. Israel was under strict orders from the Lord not to form an alliance with nearby nations lest they become a snare to them. So the Gibeonites made it look as if they were "from a far-off land." How did they do it? They positioned themselves in a misleading light to misdirect God's people, and it worked. Israel trusted what they saw, but God guided them with what they felt. The warning signs in your gut are a gift from God and a signal to seek His counsel. These promptings, or what some may call a "funny feeling," are the inward witness, where the Holy Spirit speaks to your spirit.

CHECK-IN WITH GOD

*"The warning signs in your gut are a gift from God
and a signal to seek His counsel."*
~Scott Hogle

DANGER WILL ROBINSON, DANGER! The 1960s TV Show *Lost in Space* featured a robot who yelled out, "Danger Will Robinson, Danger!" anytime young Will was close to trouble. Would you think Will was foolish if he faced danger, got a heads-up, and proceeded anyway? Yet, often, this is exactly what we do when we ignore the Lord's heart check. When our conscience smites us, like it did David in the cave with Saul, or we start to feel emotional alarm bells, that's a clue something is wrong. God is trying to protect us from someone or something He sees ahead. In Old Testament times, God's people did not have the Holy Spirit abiding in them, so they had to trust outside indicators. As a Christian, you have "Christ In You" and the voice of the Holy Spirit guiding you.

LISTEN TO YOUR INWARD WITNESS

*"The Spirit itself beareth witness with our spirit,
that we are the children of God"*
Ref. Romans 8:16.

How developed is your Spiritual Spidey sense? If you ask Spider-Man, he will tell you to "*Listen* to your Spidey-senses." It was after 5 pm one day, and I was walking down the hallway of my office, feeling frustrated. I had spent months in a corporate exercise, working on spreadsheets with my team and having what I call "a circular conversation," a conversation that doesn't go anywhere. The exercise required a lot of time, energy, and activity but produced nothing. It was driving me and my team crazy. I spent months keeping my displeasure in check, and one day, I'd had enough; I couldn't stand it anymore. It was late. I had been stewing all day in my spirit, and I decided as I walked down the hallway at the end of the day, "I've had enough; I'm going to call them and tell them what I think of this process and that I'm not doing it anymore." Suddenly, God spoke to my heart and said, "You can do that, but you'll destroy yourself." It was a direct and clear warning of what would happen if I proceeded. What was this? The inward witness was warning me about something I was about to do. I heeded the Lord's advice even though His guidance didn't make me feel any better. Years earlier, my wife Kate and I were on the North Shore of Oahu, about to hike up to see the Sacred Falls.

As we entered the path, we both got a check in our spirits that stopped us in our tracks. There was no apparent reason why; we just knew something was wrong. We stood there discussing the odd feeling that we had both just had. In the absence of clear direction, it is best to pause or stop what you are doing because God is trying to warn you, protect you from something, and give you a heads-up. We decided to leave the area and skipped the hike that day. Soon after, there was a landslide at Sacred Falls that killed a number of people; that path has been closed since. The Holy Spirit was witnessing inside of us that something wasn't quite right.

FOLLOW THE STOP LIGHT INSIDE

God has placed an internal guidance system within your heart to help you know what to do. This simple method, I call the "STOP LIGHT INSIDE," allows you to discern the right course to follow. By paying attention to this inner signal, you can avoid self-inflicted wounds. Here's an easy way to remember how God's guidance system works with your inner monitor.

RED: Red means STOP. If you are feeling anxious about a matter, it is a clear indication to STOP and turn to God. He is giving you a heads-up and warning that you are approaching danger. DO NOT PROCEED; stay out of the intersection. Philippians 4:6 instructs us to "Be anxious for nothing." So, if you are feeling anxious, this is God's sign that you should stop. Anxiousness is a STOP SIGN in your spirit.

YELLOW: Yellow means BE CAUTIOUS. It can mean proceeding cautiously, possible danger ahead, or PAUSE. For me, yellow can also mean UNCERTAINTY; approach with caution. When I am sensing a YELLOW signal in my spirit, I pause and look to the heavens. If you feel uncertain on a matter, wait until you get a green light to proceed or direction to adjust your course. I have often found that a GODLY PAUSE indicates that the timing isn't right or there is more information I will need to be successful prior to entering the intersection of decision. When you get a check in your spirit, follow your inward prompting and PAUSE.

GREEN: Green means go ahead and proceed. Colossians 3:15 reminds us to "Let the peace of Christ rule in our hearts." To rule means to "umpire" in this context. Like an umpire behind the plate calling balls or strikes, so it is with the Spirit of God within you, giving you the green light to "take your base" when there is peace. If you have "peaceful feelings" or a positive unction after seeking God on a matter, peace is your green light to proceed, to GO!

REFLECT TO CONNECT

1. God's guidance system is active within you 24/7. What do you need to seek His wisdom or guidance on today?
2. Have you ever experienced God speaking to you in a way other than through the "STOP LIGHT INSIDE" method?
3. Can you recall a time when you ignored your inward monitor and looked back as Joshua did with regret?

Imaginating with God

*"Call unto me, and I will answer thee, and show thee great
and mighty things,*

which thou knowest not" Jeremiah 33:3 (KJV).

Vision casting with God is the art of imaginating with Him to co-create the events of your future, allowing you to see what He sees. To vision cast with the Holy Spirit, you're going to need three things; your Bible, a journal, and your imagination. Your imagination is like a movie screen within your spirit. It can replay past events, visualize the unseen in the present, and envision future possibilities. While most people use their imagination automatically and habitually, there's a powerful way to use it intentionally to co-create with God. If I were to ask you to imagine your childhood home, you could easily do it. You could walk me through it and describe every room in the house: your bedroom, the living room, where you ate dinner, and where your family set up the Christmas tree. If I were to ask you to drive home from church or your workplace, you could imagine every stop sign, stop light, and every turn, even the traffic in front of you. You use your imagination to replay events from your past or pre-play events you see your future. Speakers can use their imagination to visualize themselves presenting weeks before the actual event. You can even use your imagination to role play conversations with people. Professional athletes use their imagination to play out scenarios in a game before they happen so they are better prepared. They can play an entire game in their mind's eye. When they can SEE IT, THEY CAN DO IT. The same is true for you.

SEE IT SO YOU CAN DO IT

"I can only do what I see the Father doing." Ref. John 5:19

You need a clear picture of God's Will to implement it in your life. Inviting God to use your imagination to paint a picture of His Will and forecast His future for you is what I call "IMAGINATING WITH GOD."

Meditating in God's presence and asking Him to show you what is to come is what I refer to as spending "Screen Time in the Spirit." Jesus told His disciples that the Holy Spirit would reveal future events (John 16:13-15). It is God's Will for you to hear and see His plans for your life. By showing you what He sees in your imagination, God is directing you with a picture to guide you. God guided David this way. In Psalms 32:8, God promises, *"I will instruct you and teach you in the way you should go. I will counsel you with my eye upon you."* Jesus demonstrated this by saying, "I can only do what I SEE the Father doing." Just as Jesus used His spiritual eyes to see Himself healing, speaking over people, or making clay from mud and spit, you, too, can follow this example. Visualize yourself in alignment with God's Will, seeing and then acting on what He reveals to you.

Have you ever role-played in your mind how a conversation might go with a person or how you might present a proposal or answer an objection? In your mind's eye, have you seen yourself performing, doing, or saying something you've created in your imagination? Imagine what you could accomplish by inviting God to Imaginate with you. Why not invite God to cast His vision across the screen of your imagination? God's vision casting to co-create the future started in the Old Testament.

MENTAL MOVIES

*"I will pour out my spirit upon all flesh; and your sons
and your daughters shall prophesy,
your old men shall dream dreams, your young men
shall see visions."* Joel 2:28

It's time to ask the Holy Spirit to cast a vision for your life. When God wanted to birth a dream in Abraham, He showed up at his tent and asked him to step outside, LOOK UP into the sky, and start counting the stars. What was God doing? He was giving Abraham a picture that he could meditate on. As Abraham meditated on this image, it began to incubate in his spirit. As it incubated, Abraham became pregnant with God's vision for his life. What is planted in your spirit and watered will eventually be birthed in your life. God's vision, mixed with faith, brings to pass what He promises.

A promise of God starts with a picture. When God wanted to download a plan to Jacob about how He would take Jacob from poverty to prosperity and deliver him from Laban's hand, He gave him a vision, a picture of what He was about to do. God revealed to Jacob that He would multiply the spotted and speckled cattle Jacob was tending. With this vision in mind, Jacob strategically set up a situation to reap the reward God had shown him. This insight allowed him to align his actions with God's promise. A picture God brings to you may be seen through your spiritual eyes, your imagination. The Apostle Paul prayed in Ephesians 1:18, "May the eyes of your heart be enlightened." Elisha also spoke of our spiritual eyesight when his servant saw the size of the Syrian army and was concerned that they would overpower them. To comfort his servant, Elisha prayed, "Lord, please open his eyes so that he may see that there are more with us than with them." There is an unseen world that is not visible to the naked eye.

Why is seeing with your spiritual eyes so important? Because when you can envision it and can see it, you can do it. When you have a picture of God's Will, you can implement it like Jacob did. He was taking steps in the natural to co-create what God had shown him in the spiritual. There will always be something you need to do practically to bring to pass what God is showing you spiritually. Combining the natural with the spiritual always creates something supernatural. Faith requires action; the steps you take on God's vision brings His Will for your life from the spiritual into the natural.

THE LANGUAGE OF THE HOLY SPIRIT

"But when He, the Spirit of truth, comes, He will guide you into all the truth; for He will not speak on His own, but whatever He hears, He will speak; and He will disclose to you what is to come. He will glorify Me, for He will take from Mine and will disclose it to you." John 16:13-14

It's time to start vision casting with the Holy Spirit. Pictures and scripture are the primary language of the Holy Spirit and He often uses both to SHOW you what He is doing or wants *you* to do. My brother Steve, under the direction of the Lord, started a cyber security business. Following God every step of the way, he spent most of the first year waiting for God to do or say something. When the time came, God would speak and show Steve the next steps. In Steve's first year of business, before he even had his first client, Steve was at a conference listening to a faith-filled message (scriptures) when God whispered, "Call so and so." Steve did, and they became his first client. In his second year of business, Steve was at another conference, listening to an inspiring word about the Pearl of Great Price. Steve had a question posed to his heart, "Where is the gold in my field?" God gave Steve a picture of someone from his past that he should call. Steve made that call, and they became a large client for him that year. What was Steve experiencing? The language of the Holy Spirit where God spoke to him with scriptures while he sat in his seat, as well as a picture of who God would use to answer his prayer.

When I am vision-casting with the Holy Spirit and asking God to help me set goals or plan for the future, I often ask him for a picture or a scripture. In one instance, I asked God to give me a picture, and He gave me a picture of an airplane landing. It made no sense to me… but then again, the things of the spirit are often foolishness to the natural mind (1 Corinthians 2:14). I have trained my mind to remember that when God gives me something that doesn't make sense, I need to sit on it. Just as the Holy Spirit HOVERED over the deep at creation, I, too, hover over a word or picture God has given me. As I do, I am IMAGINATING WITH GOD, incubating on a God-given picture of scripture to see how He may expand or unpack it for me. Like a mother hen sitting on her eggs, you, too, are to meditate on the picture, scripture, or verse God has given you. As you meditate, you will be incubating and giving God the spiritual working materials to bring to pass what He has promised. It is a process that unfolds over time.

AIRPLANES AND OBSTACLE COURSES

Since God gave me a picture of an airplane landing, I saw it in my imagination and wanted to find a picture that matched what I imagined. I Googled images of airplanes landing until I found one that fit and printed it out. I have that picture of the plane landing on a small runway in my office, journal, and other places where I can see it frequently. I put it in places where I'll see it regularly so I can meditate on it and ask God questions about it. A few months later, while having lunch with my wife and a business associate, I felt prompted to share the picture with her. This particular business associate had a background in dance. When I told her the story of the airplane landing, she said, "How you land determines how you take off." It is a fundamental lesson taught to dancers. Although I found this interesting, it did not give me any further insight into how God was using this particular picture to birth a new vision for my life. But as God does in His perfect timing, shortly after that luncheon, God whispered in my spirit, "You are about to land on your calling." God will often give us a piece at a time. You may stay pregnant for a long time with a vision of what God is planning. For Abraham, he counted the stars for twenty-five years before having Issac. To this day, God's vision for Abraham is still reproducing. The bigger the vision, the longer the runway for it to take off. What picture might God be bringing to you?

Knowing the language of the Holy Spirit, I bring my problems and challenges into my quiet time to co-create and Imaginate solutions with God. I will ask God to show me what I should do, or sometimes I will ask him to show me what is unseen. I have learned to bring everything into my quiet time. Sometimes, I sit there with my eyes closed and ask God to open the eyes of my heart to show me what I need to know. Sometimes, I get an idea, a word, a whisper, or a picture. Sometimes, I get nothing, but an answer materializes later in the day or week. It is not a perfect process, and remember that we prophesy in part (1 Corinthians 13:9). There will be times you will be right and times you will be wrong. The scripture encourages us, over and over again, to test every spirit, that every word from Him should be confirmed by two or three witnesses. It is the law of confirmation.

GOD'S WORD OF THE YEAR

Vision may come to you in a word. One year, I asked God to give me a word for the year. People in business often choose a word to symbolize what they've experienced or what they're striving or hoping for in the upcoming year. Near the end of the year, I ask God to give me His word for my upcoming year, a word that symbolizes where He is leading me. In that word, God is vision-casting with me, for me. Sometimes, He also gives my wife a word of the year. Recently, He gave my wife the word, unlocked. Wow, what an exciting word!

The word God gave me that year was perseverance; I was not so excited about that word. After all, who gets excited about going into a season of testing where they have to struggle, strive, and stretch their faith? God was giving me a heads-up about the obstacle course I was about to enter. He showed me that it would take perseverance to make it through that race.

That year would be one of the most difficult I would ever experience, but God was with me every step of the way. Halfway through that year, God said to me, "I am going to put you under pressure to see how deep your well is." When God speaks to you, He will often speak in a tone similar to your self-talk voice but different in words. I knew what this meant. He wasn't putting me under pressure so He could determine how deep my well was; in His foreknowledge, He knows my limits. He was putting me under pressure so *I* could discover how deep my well was and how strong or weak my perseverance muscle was.

God wanted to give me reference points through struggling and persevering, so as I went to the next season and faced great difficulty, those reference points would become standing stones and anchors I could hold on to in the storms I would later face. God did the same thing for David when David killed the lion in the bear. That victory became a reference point, so when King Saul told David he could not win in a battle with Goliath, David replied with a reference point by saying, "I killed the lion and the bear, and this Philistine will be no different."

What one word might symbolize where God is leading you in this next season? God's plan to grow you up in your faith may require a season of difficulty. A clear word, picture, or scripture will give you the strength to stay the course.

REFLECT TO CONNECT

1. In what practical ways do you use your imagination on a daily basis?
2. Is there a problem you can bring into your quiet time to seek God's help with?
3. As you ask God to give you a vision of what's ahead, is there a picture or word that comes to mind?

A Sure Word in Season

"And thine ears shall hear a word behind thee, saying,
This is the way, walk ye in it; when ye turn to the right hand,
and when ye turn to the left" Isaiah 30:21.

Have you ever checked in with God and then changed plans? David spent the early years of his career in the military. Scripture repeatedly says of David, *"And David inquired of the Lord."* On one occasion, after delivering the city from an enemy, David was stationed at Keilah. He got word that King Saul was planning to kill him, so he checked in with God. He asked the Lord, "Will the citizens of Keilah hand me and my men over to Saul?" And the LORD replied, *"They will hand you over."* Based on this information, David chose to remove himself and his men from harm. In God's foreknowledge, He saw into the future. David acted wisely by seeking God's guidance, and God gave him a heads-up, prompting him to alter his plans. This illustrates that God's foreknowledge does not dictate destiny; you have choices. Getting a SURE WORD IN SEASON is critical to stay on course. While you will be unsure of the Will of God at times, God is always sure about what you should do. God always knows what you should say and do in every circumstance. While you live "in-time," He lives in eternity and sees the beginning and end of every situation in your life. In His foreknowledge, He can give you answers and a heads-up on something coming your way so you can adapt to it or get out of the way.

"A SURE WORD from the Lord is like handlebars for your faith; it gives you something to hang onto when circumstances are otherwise." ~ Scott Hogle

GOD MATH VS. MAN MATH

"A word spoken in due season, how good it is!" Proverbs 15:23

With a SURE WORD, I have decided to buy cars, homes, and invest in property. With a SURE WORD, I have said yes to one path of medical treatment and no to medical surgery; you could say I have bet my life on the Word of the Lord. With a SURE WORD, I make daily decisions that guide my path, some big and some small. A SURE WORD is not a guess; it's more than an informed opinion; it is a direction from God on what to do for your specific situation. Scripture says, *"You have not because you ask not."* God desires you to seek him, and in your seeking, He promises to be found by you. Nothing pleases the Lord more than when you intentionally set your heart to pursue and involve Him in your daily doings. In fact, God said it this way in Proverbs 3:5-6, *"Trust in the LORD with all your heart and do not lean on your own understanding. In all your ways acknowledge Him, and He will make your paths straight."* God's SURE WORD to you may not always make sense to your natural mind, but you will have peace and confidence, a sure-footedness of where to step and what to do. When God speaks to you, it is important that you do not do the math.

Let me explain. Guidance from God is for your direction, not deliberation. God is not guessing or figuring out the pluses and minuses of a situation. We do that with our natural mind, but when it comes to receiving answers from God, they are received, not calculated. Years ago, my wife Kate and I felt led to partner with God in an investment property for ministry use. The plan was to buy a property missionaries would use for foster care, lease it back to them at a loss, and one day sell it, believing God would take care of us on the back end. A person in business would tell you that this is not a sound financial strategy, but we were banking on God's math.

THE LAW OF CONFIRMATION

"Beloved, do not believe every spirit, but test the spirits to see whether they are from God, because many false prophets have gone out into the world." 1 John 4:1

Other people will confirm the Word of the Lord when you seek God. Ray, a missionary friend, and I spent a year looking at hundreds of properties online, but nothing was quite right. On this particular day, I stumbled upon the perfect property. God's answers often come "all of a sudden." I called Ray to look at what I had found, and it turned out that Ray had seen the same property and knew that "it was the one." How is it possible that Ray and I would struggle for a year to find the right property and then zero in on the same property on the same day, with thousands of searches 365 days later? That can only be the Lord. You will not always be right when hearing from God; there can be interferences in the heavenly realm. Interference can come in the form of spiritual warfare, as it did when

Daniel's answer to prayer was delayed 21 days, or it could be interference from your own spirit. There may be personal desires that muddy the waters. There are a few ways to confirm whether or not something is coming from the Lord. The Word of the Lord will never contradict God's Word or character. You will have peace and no anxiety about the Word of the Lord for your circumstances. And the Law of Confirmation will be at work, *"Let every word be confirmed by two or more witnesses."* A confirmation from God may come through a person, place, or circumstance, and it will be ultimately confirmed with a sense of PEACE and FULL ASSURANCE on the inside of you, deep within your spirit. You will KNOW IN YOUR KNOWER with certainty that you have received a SURE WORD.

IS THAT REALLY YOU GOD?

"For the Word of God is living and active, and sharper than any two-edged sword, even penetrating as far as the division of soul and spirit, of both joints and marrow, and able to judge the thoughts and intentions of the heart." Hebrews 4:12

The founder of Youth With A Mission, Loren Cunningham, wrote a book years ago called, *Is That Really You, God?* One of the ways he describes how missionaries would receive confirmation as they prayed to the Lord for counsel is to pray together and then share what God had said to each one of them. If God was giving multiple people the same message, it is a confirmation, "a word that had been confirmed by two or three witnesses." Praying with a trusted friend who hears from God can be helpful when looking for a sure word in season. Who do you know that you could pray with today?

When God speaks, JUST DO IT! We made the offer through a realtor, and I was off to Florida to attend a John Maxwell Team certification conference. While there, a call came in informing us that we had been outbid on the property in Las Vegas. The next day, I was driving down the highway, and a torrential rain started. The sky opened up, and the rain fell so fast and furious that I couldn't see the road and had to pull over. Sitting on the side of the road in my rental car, I began to pray and then cry. After years of looking and leaning into the Lord for His guidance, I was upset that we had been wrong about the property we had found. I was more upset that I had missed God than over losing the property. I was about to call Ray when I heard God's voice, "Go to Las Vegas." That was it, nothing more. I thought, "I don't like Las Vegas; I just want to go home." God's voice to you will sound like your own but different. It comes from within your born-again spirit where His Spirit dwells and bubbles up to your mind where you receive understanding. I have found God's SURE WORD is direct, flat, and always soft-spoken, almost as a whisper. How does God's voice sound in your spirit when He speaks to you?

DOING BUSINESS WITH GOD

*"My sheep hear my voice, and I know them,
and they follow me."* John 10:27

What do you do when you hear God right, but it doesn't pan out? Stay the course and do what God is telling you to do. Feeling like I was wrong already in hearing His voice, I figured I had nothing to lose if I went to Las Vegas and looked like a fool. So, I changed my plane ticket to fly from West Palm,

Florida, to Las Vegas and booked a hotel for one night. The next day, the conference ended, and I was on the plane listening to worship music and thinking about the things of God. Escaping into God's presence by worshiping through your crisis is oftentimes the best medicine. It wasn't God I was doubting; it was me I couldn't trust after thinking I heard wrong. When the plane landed, my phone showed a voicemail had come in during the flight. The realtor said, "The other buyer backed out, and the property will still be yours if you want it." I rented a car, drove straight to her office, and signed the papers. "Go to Las Vegas" didn't make sense when God spoke it, but I have learned that God's promptings and SURE WORD will not always line up with what you see in the present moment; follow them anyway. God's Word may be telling you one thing when your circumstance says another. FOLLOW ANYWAY.

GOD'S SURE WORD LEADS TO FRUITFULNESS

Through the missionaries work on that property, many kids were helped and placed with Christian Foster Care families. When that season drew to an end, and the missionaries were called to leave Las Vegas, I faced a decision to sell or rent the property. I asked the Lord, and He said, "Rent it and see what I will do." We rented the property for a couple of years, and when that tenant left, God prompted us to sell it. The market was red hot, and we expected an offer to sell quickly. Our realtor was so confident it would sell that very first weekend. Three months later, we still didn't have even one offer. Something was off. I KNEW IN MY KNOWER that I had heard from God, but the results did not "pan out" the way I thought they would.

What was wrong? In hindsight, I know now that God was waiting for me to come to Him and ask for His counsel! I was being trained to seek Him not once but each step of the way. So I did. In prayer, I walked boldly into the Throne Room of Grace to state my case. Humbly, yet with confidence, I said to God, "I did what you told me to do and it's not working out." I wish I could tell you that God said something when I prayed, but He didn't. Yet I knew my situation had now been put in His hands and would be handled. Within a week, we received an offer at the full list price. We didn't make much money renting it, but it sold for almost twice what we paid. Without knowing how to receive a SURE WORD in season, we would have missed an important piece of our Divine Destiny. Lessons learned in that season have served us well for years. When seeking God's SURE WORD in season for my situations, I am comforted to know that my life decisions go through His hands.

REFLECT TO CONNECT

1. What do you need a SURE WORD from God about in this season?
2. How has God confirmed His direction for your life in the past?
3. Has God ever given you a SURE WORD for your circumstance that you didn't like? What did you do?

The Problem with Money

*"But you are to remember the LORD your God, for it is
He who is giving you power to make wealth, in order to
confirm His covenant which He swore to your fathers,
as it is this day"* Deuteronomy 8:18.

Money is good! It's okay for you to want, need, and
desire it. In fact, most people do. Money is a necessary
tool for living, attaining, getting ahead, and moving the
Kingdom of God forward. God doesn't object to you having
money or significant sums. Yet He *is* concerned with your
stewardship of it. Scripture is clear that *"The love of money is
the root of all evil,"* but money, by itself, is not. With that said,
God cares deeply about how you let money influence your
heart. If you're not careful, money can twist your motives
and lead you astray. I've seen it happen—money can turn
a heart and take someone off course. Money has a way of
drawing our hearts away from God if you don't guard against
it, but it can also draw your heart toward Him. Jesus said in
Matthew 6:21, *"For where your treasure is, there will also be
your heart."* This means the influence money has over your
heart can be used to TURN YOUR HEART toward God.
How do you do this? By investing your money in eternity
and into the people and purposes of God where moth and

rust won't destroy. How has the Lord guided you to invest in eternity?

In the International bestselling Devotional, *Divine Intelligence*, I wrote about how some Christians are SHAMED FOR SUCCESS in the church. Sadly, many wrong teachings about money shame people for the size of their success or the size of their bank accounts. Some have even stopped going to church because they felt guilty for being well-off. If you believe that money is good and can be used to advance yourself, your family, and God's purposes, keep reading.

GOD-GOGGLES

"What will be done for the man who kills this Philistine and rids Israel of the disgrace?"
1 Samuel 17:26

When you see it, you can seize it! God owns the cattle on a thousand hills but has no money. If you pray for mailbox money to magically appear, you will be waiting a long time. There is a better way for you to improve your situation, God's way, with His help. How does God help you? He directs you where to go and where to look. By putting on God-Goggles to see a situation as He sees it, your eyes are open to opportunities you may have missed. He opens your eyes to identify opportunities that already exist around you; that is His specialty. Seeing through God-Goggles means viewing a situation as God sees it. For 40 days, the Israeli army lined up against the Philistine army, paralyzed in fear. Each day, Goliath, a ten-foot giant, would challenge Israel to settle the fight by sending their best warrior to face him, but not one accepted the challenge. When young David showed up to the battlefield to bring food to his older brothers, he did not see through the eyes of fear as the Israeli warriors did; he saw financial opportunity. Where the army of Israel saw an impossible situation, David saw an income-making opportunity.

When you see something and have a strong emotional reaction opposite to others, it's a clue that God is revealing something others are blind to. When others shrink back, your spirit rises up, and God is urging you to handle the problem in front of you. Looking through his God-Goggles, young David turned a problem into a big payday. After seeing what was going on, David's opportunity radar had turned on and he asked, "What will be done for the man who kills this Philistine and rids Israel of the disgrace?" The answer to this question motivated David, and he seized the opportunity. David wasn't only thinking spiritually; he was thinking financially. He wanted to know what reward he would receive once he rid Israel of this problem. David was told that the king would make the victor a rich man, give his daughter to wed, and the problem solver would not have to pay taxes again (Ref. 1 Samuel 17:25-26). Wow, what a moment of opportunity for David. So when faced with a challenge, he saw as God saw and stepped up where others stepped down. When you put on your God-Goggles of Opportunity, you will see the hidden opportunities God presents.

Here is how your perspective will change when you look at your situation with God-Goggles:

- Where others shrink back in fear, you rise up in faith.
- Where others see a dead end, you see a <u>doorway</u>.

- Where others see a setback, you see a <u>setup for success</u>.
- Where others see a problem, you see <u>potential and possibilities</u>.
- When others step down, you step up and seize <u>God's open door to your Divine Destiny</u>.

GOD-GOGGLES WILL CHANGE YOUR PERSPECTIVE

*"What would you attempt to do if you knew
you could not fail?"* ~Robert Schuller

Two Christian shoe salesmen were sent to Africa to open a new territory. One phoned home a week later and said, "No one here wears shoes; everyone walks around with bare feet. There is no opportunity HERE; I will be home next week." The other called the company headquarters with a different message, "No one HERE wears shoes; they all walk bare feet. Opportunity is EVERYWHERE. I won't be home for a long time." What was the difference between the two shoe salesmen? One saw a dead end; the other saw a doorway to huge opportunity in an undeveloped area.

Both salesmen were praying for success, hoping, wishing, and praying that God would show up and help them. One saw an obstacle; the other saw a God-sized opportunity. Stephen Covey once said, "We see the world not as it is, but as we are— or as we are conditioned to see it." When you face a challenge or difficulty, do you see an obstacle or an opportunity? To see as God sees, you have to put on your God-Goggles. How often have you prayed for something and then waited, waited, and waited some more? Then, when the answer finally came, you realized it was there all along. In my bestselling business book

Persuade, I share the story of the LAW OF THE PROSPECTOR. The story was written by Russell Conwell, and it is one of the most motivational stories told in the last century. The story illustrates that when you train yourself to look for opportunity rather than obstacles, you will realize that the opportunity you seek is likely right under your feet, within your reach. *Opening your eyes to see what God has already provided is where answers to prayer start.*

OPPORTUNITY IS UNDER YOUR FEET

*"We are all faced with a series of great opportunities,
brilliantly disguised as impossible situations."*
~Charles R. Swindoll

Automotive advertising is one of the biggest spending categories in television and radio. After going into a new market, I was surprised to learn that very few auto dealers advertised on the radio. When asked why, I was told that auto dealers don't use radio in the city. This was code for saying that calling automotive dealers to advertise on the radio was a dead end. Where others saw a dead end, I saw a doorway. My friend James and I began calling on auto dealers and, within a few years, had grown the category from nothing to $2,000,000 a year in revenue. Did we create the revenue out of thin air? No, it was always there, hiding within reach, under our feet. How many people spend years praying that God would increase their paychecks, but they fail to develop the potential right under their feet? What opportunity is within your reach that you have not seized yet?

*"I will give you the treasures of darkness and hidden wealth
of secret places, So that you may know that it is I, The LORD,
the God of Israel, who calls you by your name."* Isaiah 45:3

ACRES OF DIAMONDS

*"And my God will supply all your needs according to
His riches in glory in Christ Jesus."* Philippians 4:19

Acres of Diamonds is a story of a farmer living on the continent
of Africa who heard tales of other farmers making millions
discovering diamond mines. The tales excited the farmer so
much that he sold his farm to go prospecting for diamonds
himself. After searching in hopes of discovering his own field
of wealth, he was unsuccessful and gave up. Thinking he had
wasted all of his resources, he threw himself into a river and
drowned. Meanwhile, the young farmer who bought his ranch
was walking his new property when he noticed a sparkle of
light gleaming up at him from the bed of a stream. He bent
down and picked up the sparkling stone. It was a good-sized
one, and admiring it, he brought it home and put it on the
mantle of his fireplace. A friend, while visiting him sometime
later, noticed the stone and picked it up for a closer look. He
almost fainted from the weight and look of the stone. The
friend asked the farmer if he knew what he'd found. When
the farmer said he thought it was a nice rock, the visitor told
him that he had discovered one of the largest diamonds ever.
Later, this proved to be true. The farmer stood in disbelief and
told his friend that the bottom of his stream was full of similar-
looking stones. The first farmer sold everything he had and set
out to prospect for his own opportunity. The second farmer

discovered an acre of diamonds already within his reach. His newly discovered acre of diamonds already belonged to him; he just had to notice the riches that were already there. The first farmer's property turned out to be one of the most productive diamond mines on the African continent. Earl Nightingale, in his version of *Acres of Diamonds,* observed that "The first farmer had owned free and clear, acres of diamonds. But he had sold them for practically nothing, in order to look elsewhere. The moral is clear: If the first farmer had only taken the time to study and learn what diamonds looked like in their rough state and to thoroughly explore the property he had before looking elsewhere, all of his wildest dreams would have come true."

Acres of Diamonds has always been one of my favorite stories because it reveals multiple hidden meanings. Looking through God-Goggles, you realize God has already provided what you need (Philippians 4:19). I often ask God, "Lord, please open my eyes to see what is hidden, what is within my reach." Looking through God-Goggles, you will start to spot God-sized opportunities in their undeveloped state. Why are they in an undeveloped state like the rough-cut diamonds from the story? Because God is hiding them from others for you. He hides opportunities within reach, so when you see them, you can seize them. The opportunity you seek is within reach, likely under your feet.

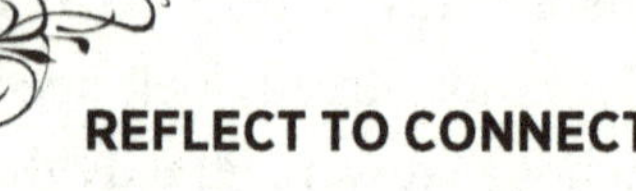

REFLECT TO CONNECT

1. As you pray and ask to see how God sees your situation, what do you see through your God-Goggles?
2. When has your perspective changed in the past because you received new information?
3. How might our biases get in the way of seeing what God wants us to see?

Stewarding the Call

*"Like a city that is broken into and without walls,
so is a person who has no self-control over his spirit"*
Proverbs 25:28.

Elijah was one of the greatest prophets in the Bible, yet he resigned from his post. Why? Fear and fatigue. Following one of the most remarkable mountaintop experiences in his ministry, he fell into fear and despair when a woman named Jezebel threatened his life. In the season following, God would try to counsel him, and when God could no longer persuade Elijah to stay the course, He told Elijah to get Elisha to replace him. Mike Murdock, author and evangelist, once remarked, "When fatigue walks in, faith walks out." Have you noticed how quickly your faith and perseverance meter go down when you are fatigued? In today's fast-paced work environment, stress and burnout are ever-present threats that can derail even the most dedicated leaders. Without incorporating self-care and regular restoration into our daily routines, we risk reaching our breaking point. At church, we often joke, "Part-time is full-time, and full-time is all the time." While it may sound humorous, this sentiment rings true whether you work in ministry or the marketplace. It would be funnier if it weren't so true. Stewarding your time, energy, and bandwidth is critical for keeping your energy stores high and your faith full.

In 2023, hurricane winds blew over Lahaina, Maui at 60 M.P.H. Fires spread a mile a minute, and people were doing everything possible to stay out of the fire's path. In the days during and following the Maui Wild Fires, the flow of information and updates was non-stop and necessary. People needed to stay informed, and in some cases, radio was the only form of communication in Lahaina because power lines, cell towers, and fiber optics had burned to the ground. For people in the news business, many micro and macro decisions were made on a minute-by-minute basis. It was "For such a time as this" that people needed to be at their best because lives depended on it, and speed was crucial.

Have you been up late at night with your mind racing, unable to settle yourself down? As President of iHeart Radio in Hawaii, I was knee-deep in decision-making and sharing information with my company on the mainland as the Maui Fires became the central national news story that week. By the end of the week, I was running on empty. With little sleep for three days, it was midnight. I was exhausted, yet my mind was racing. I couldn't settle down even though that was what I needed most. After days of high stress and constant pressure, I was fatigued and headed for burnout. I couldn't think straight; my bandwidth was exhausted. I struggled to control my emotions and control my thought life. So I prayed, "Lord, why can't I sleep?" God gave me this scripture, *"Like a city broken into without walls, so is a person who doesn't have control over their own spirit."* I knew my mind was constantly racing, and my body was tense, so I prayed again and asked, "What do I do?". The Lord replied, *"Take every thought captive to the obedience of Christ,"* so I did. It took me a while to wrestle my thought life to the ground. I focused my thoughts on one scripture, and each time my mind drifted, I wrestled it back to meditating on that one scripture. Within a few minutes, I arrested each thought as it entered my mind and submitted it to the cross. Guiding each thought that entered my neural net into the hands of Christ, I was able to find peace and eventually fall asleep.

YOU NEED TO BE ABLE TO SUBDUE
YOUR THOUGHT LIFE

Most people don't know how to control their thought life. The mind makes a great servant when subdued but a lousy master if left alone. Your thoughts need to be managed, and ONLY YOU can manage them. It's possible with practice, and God has provided a way. Taking each thought captive to make it submissive to scripture (the word of Christ) is a sure way to ensure your mind is serving you and *you are not a slave to the motor in your mind.* Practically speaking, doing this exercise builds up your <u>mental concentration muscle,</u> which is weakened by multi-tasking, scanning, and surfing the digital universe. As you read and meditate on the Word of God to strengthen your mental concentration muscle, your thought life is brought into subjection to the Word of God, and you have control again. It is God's design that your WILL (volition) controls your thought life, not your mind, emotions, and physical senses. I find myself returning to this practice a few times a year when stress and strained bandwidth cause me to enter burnout. Each time I do, my mind gets quiet, and I am back abiding in Christ.

PSALM WALKING TO FILL YOUR TANK

"Be filled with the Spirit, speaking to one another in psalms and hymns and spiritual songs, singing and making melody with your hearts to the Lord." Ref. Ephesians 5:19-20

The week of the fires felt overwhelming, and I knew I needed a PSALM WALK. What is a Psalm walk? I keep the Psalms audio on my phone, and instead of Prayer Walking in the morning, I listen to the Psalms. Sometimes, my walk turns into a run as I let the WORD WASH OVER MY MIND. Washing your mind with the Psalms is a way to wrestle your thought life into subjection. The next time you need to enter and remain in the presence of God for an extended period, try Psalm Walking and let the word wash over your mind. It will refresh your mind, body, and spirit.

SELF-CARE FOR YOUR DIVINE DESTINY

"You will keep him in perfect peace, whose mind is stayed on you, because he trusts in you." Isaiah 26:3 (NKJV)

Let the WORD wash your mind. Did you know you are made up of mind, body, and spirit (1 Thessalonians 5:23)? God expects us to steward each part of our being. When we lose balance and life's pressures deplete our mental, emotional, and physical reserves, we risk experiencing short- or long-term burnout. This imbalance can lead to saying the wrong things, making poor choices, and creating chaos in our lives. God has empowered you to care for your mind, body, and spirit and will not do it for you. What God has given you to manage, you and you alone are responsible for stewarding. An important principle to remember is that God will not do something *for* you that He has empowered *you* to do for yourself. God's sabbath is His design for self-care. If you find yourself depleted and running on empty, return to a day of rest to ensure you are resting and recovering.

Stewarding your Divine Destiny requires that you nurture your mind, body, and spirit. Thankfully, God has empowered us to do this very thing through rest, recovery, a regular sabbath, and the Word of God.

REFLECT TO CONNECT

1. Where do you go when you need to retreat and recover?
2. What do you find restores your mind, body, and spirit?
3. How is God leading you to steward your calling?

God's Brave Hearts

"Now before the spies lay down, she came up to them on the roof, and said to the men, 'I know that the LORD has given you the land and that the terror of you has fallen on us, and that all the inhabitants of the land have despaired because of you. For <u>we have heard</u> how the LORD dried up the water of the Red Sea before you when you came out of Egypt, and what you did to the two kings of the Amorites who were beyond the Jordan, to Sihon and Og, whom you utterly destroyed'" Joshua 2:8-10.

When the two spies arrived at Jericho, Rahab didn't hesitate to hide and protect them. She took them in and chose to trust them. But it wasn't just them she was trusting; she had heard of the God of Israel and knew they were there to carry out His Will. Rahab had great faith because she KNEW OF and HEARD of the God who was leading Israel. *"Faith comes by HEARING and HEARING by the Word of God"* (Romans 10:17). When faith rises up within you, you become a BRAVE HEART. You will see, act, and perceive in the natural what God is stirring in the spiritual. Rahab risked her life, but it wasn't a reckless gamble. She was betting on the character of God. Even though she didn't witness the Red Sea parting firsthand, she had unwavering confidence in what was coming. What you see, hear, or sense on the outside will be affirmed by a strong conviction within. This is how you'll KNOW God is at work. Faith is rising up.

THE HALL OF FAITH

"For by it the people of old gained approval. By faith the prostitute Rahab did not perish along with those who were disobedient, after she had welcomed the spies in peace . . . And what more shall I say? For time will fail me if I tell of Gideon, Barak, Samson, Jephthah, of David and Samuel and the prophets, who by faith conquered kingdoms, performed acts of righteousness, obtained promises, shut the mouths of lions, quenched the power of fire, escaped the edge of the sword, from weakness were made strong, became mighty in war, put foreign armies to flight" Hebrews 11:2, 31-34.

What will your story be in the Hall of Faith when the books are opened? Rehab was strong, bold, and courageous when the King of Jericho questioned her. She took a step of courage and in that one decision, she became God's BRAVE HEART. Instead of turning the Israelite spies over, she hid them on her roof, risking her life by putting her trust in God. If things didn't work out, she would surely die. This moment of faith-driven decision defined her, saved her and her family, and grafted her into the family of God. Rahab is celebrated as a great Woman of Faith in Hebrew 11. Who are the Rahabs, the brave hearts, in your life?

GREAT WOMEN OF FAITH AND COURAGE

My mother, Helen, is a great woman of faith who describes herself as having "a passive faith." What she calls passive, I see as a steadfast trust in God's provision. Like Rehab, she grew up hearing of God's greatness in a household of faithful parents. She's had a can-do attitude, was always positive and prayerful, and tirelessly worked day and night to provide for her family.

She worked as if everything depended on her and trusted God for the rest. There were many times she had to bravely trust in the invisible providential hand of God in times of financial crisis.

One woman's BRAVE HEART leaves a legacy to live up to. Helen often tells stories about those times when there was "too much month at the end of the money." When bills were due but there was no money, she prayed for provision. Her prayers were answered in unexpected ways. When our old beat-up car was hit, the damage led to a cash payout. When an old shed in the backyard was destroyed in a storm, she ran an ad in the paper, and a man who needed the wood removed it for free, and the insurance company sent a check. When we needed a new roof, a tree branch fell through the roof in a storm, and insurance covered the cost of our new roof. One year, just before Christmas, as she was preparing to host her Sunday school class, she prayed, "Lord, this carpet is so old and shabby." While her Sunday school class made candles, one of them fell onto the carpet and caught on fire. Can you guess what happened next? The insurance company provided new carpet and paint, and she got a new living room. Another time, there was a hail storm the size of golf balls that destroyed the siding on the house. You can guess what happened next. At one point, she felt guilty using her insurance to cover these strange events, but the insurance company reassured her, "This is why you have insurance." We decide what to pray; God decides how our prayers will be answered. In what ways might God be answering your prayers in unconventional ways? When circumstances are otherwise, you may need to bravely put your trust in God like Rahab and Helen did. When you are facing this decision, it is God inviting you to be a BRAVE HEART. Helen's faith is a testament to trusting God's timing and provision, showing how a steadfast belief can turn challenges into blessings.

BRAVE HEARTS SERVE THE PURPOSES OF GOD

You may be thrust into a situation where you are forced to be brave in order to survive. This may be an invitation for you to deepen your trust in the Lord. My mother's mother, Olga, was taken from her home in Ukraine when she was 15 by the Germans and forced to work in camps during World War II. Olga persevered through these horrific times and later became an interpreter between the Germans and the Ukrainians. God gave Olga a gift for understanding languages. You could say she was a go-between, a mediator. The Americans eventually liberated Olga and her people from the German work camps and placed them in refugee camps. There, she met my grandfather, Paul. They set out to start their new life in Australia and had a date to set sail when my grandmother suddenly fell ill, and they missed their ship. Through a twist of fate, their plans changed, and they were now set to sail instead to America. In her generation, she, too, would serve the purposes of God, raise a family, and, like Rehab, play a pivotal role in spreading God's word in her country. Their mission was not just a personal journey but a significant contribution to their community. She and her husband served in the Ukrainian Baptist church in America, working as worship leaders and eventually missionaries who would return to Ukraine before the Iron Curtain fell to preach and smuggle bibles into underground churches. Like Rehab, her decision to follow God would graft her into a position where she became a matriarch of difference makers, committed to the cause of Christ. As Rehab and Salmon gave birth to Boaz, who married Ruth and became the ancestor of Obed, Jesse, David, and eventually, Jesus, Olga's decision to become a BRAVE HEART for Christ grafted her a lineage of God's followers. In God's providence, Olga and her husband have produced teachers, preachers, singers, worship leaders, and apostolic broadcasters who advance the Gospel in America and around the world, serving God in their generation.

Is there a woman who exhibits bravery and perseverance in serving God's purposes who has inspired you? Someone you can follow after? Perhaps you are the person God wants to raise up as the first in your family and generation to become God's Brave Heart.

WHO IS THE INSPIRING WOMAN OF FAITH IN YOUR LIFE?

"He who finds a wife finds a good thing, and obtains favor from the LORD." Proverbs 18:22

A great woman of faithfulness and courage is my wife, Kate. She embodies the devotion of Ruth, the wisdom and bravery of Abigail, the brilliance and business savvy of Lydia, and a commitment to the call of Christ like Priscilla. She calls herself a "Cliff Jumper for Jesus." To be a Cliff Jumper for Jesus, decisions to take bold and brave steps must become a lifestyle. When God prompted Kate to quit her job and give up a six-figure income to start a business, she did. After the jump,

God met her, and today, she runs one of the most successful advertising agencies in the city. When she lost one of her biggest accounts, her response wasn't worry; it was, "This is God's business. God's got this." It takes a brave heart not to worry in the face of great loss. When a big cable company asked Kate to train their sales staff for two days, she said yes, although she had never trained other people in sales before. She prayed, prepared herself, and walked in faith, knowing God would be with her. That takes guts. When I was diagnosed with cancer, she interceded until God gave her a SURE WORD that He would take care of it. Kate, too, is committed to serving the purposes of God in her generation. For decades, she has served in women's ministry, modeled Christ in the marketplace, and exhibited Christ's grace and kindness to a world in need of both. She is the bravest woman I know, not because she is brave but because she faces her fears by walking through them in faith. If you were to ask Kate why she doesn't fear, she would tell you, "It's because I know who is walking by my side." She knows God is there when she needs Him, and she puts His Will above her worries. One of the things all great women of faith share is their role as intercessors for their families and future generations. It is not a responsibility exclusive to them but one we all share. Who has God placed on your heart today? Whose lives can you impact through your prayers and intercession?

When you meet a BRAVE HEART, you know it. God's Brave Hearts headed for the Hall of Faith in their generation radiate the glory of God, and they possess peace, strength, and patience that can only come from a deep-rooted faith. They have learned to suffer and sacrifice for their calling, serving Christ with their lives devoted to an audience of One, yearning to one day hear, "Well done, good and faithful servant." Their lives are a testament to the power of faith in overcoming life's greatest challenges, facing giants along the way, overcoming obstacles, and persevering through the impossible. They, too, like Rahab, have entered the Hall of Faith in their generation. They are God's Brave Hearts.

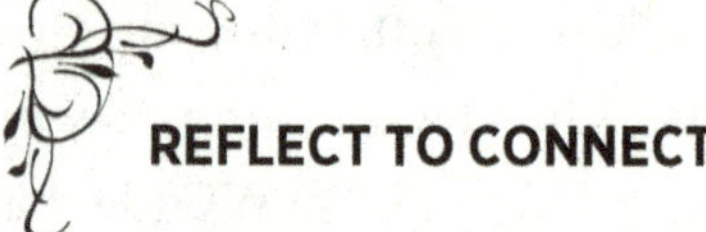

REFLECT TO CONNECT

1. Who in your Hall of Faith has inspired you to follow their example?
2. Is there a great woman of faith you can show appreciation to today?
3. What are some of the qualities God gives to a woman that are different than those he gives to a man?

Healed of Cancer

*"This is what the LORD, the God of your father, David says,
'I have heard your prayer, I have seen your tears; behold, I
am going to heal you. On the third day, you shall go up to the
house of the LORD. And I will add fifteen years to your life'"*
Ref. 2 Kings 20:5-6.

This scripture holds deep meaning for me because God gave it to me during my battle for survival. After deciding to go "all in" and trust God for my healing, I remember telling my friend Lance, "If I go down, I go down, but I will go down trusting God." How did this practically play out? My story follows, but first, I'd like to share how God used one courageous woman's story to help me on my healing journey.

BETTING YOUR LIFE ON GOD

Dodie Osteen wrote an inspiring book titled *Healed of Cancer* that chronicled her extraordinary journey. I read it in one sitting during my battle with cancer, and faith rose up in me for healing. Dodie went into the hospital with symptoms, and the doctors pronounced her death sentence. While the doctor declared one thing, she and her husband, John, were proclaiming another. When the doctor said this was the end, she proclaimed it was the beginning, and they began to pray. During her journey, there were two things Dodie did that inspired me. When God brings an inspiring example into your life, it is God's way of saying, "This is for you too." Dodie posted scriptures of God's promises for healing all over her room so she would be reminded, day and night, of God's promises of healing. She also posted pictures of herself from a time when she was young and strong. Why did she do this? Because what you see and behold on the outside eventually imprints on the inside. Early in my cancer journey, I was spending a lot of time in bed because cancer had eaten the bottom of the bones inside my leg. For months, I struggled to walk, shower, and get up to go to the bathroom at night. Living a sickly lifestyle eventually changes how you see and think about yourself. After reading Dodie's story, the Lord led me to pull out pictures of myself when I was young, vibrant, and full of strength. One of those pictures was my High School varsity football picture. When I looked at that picture, it REMINDED ME of a time in my life when I had endless energy, could run like the wind, and felt bulletproof. Until you change the picture on the inside of you, you will be tied to your circumstances on the outside.

You read earlier in IMAGINATE WITH GOD that what you incubate in your inward spirit will eventually produce an outward circumstance. After meditating on the pictures and promises of God, He led me to a new image, a substance of faith, and the image that was forming was the evidence of the things not seen. The definition of FAITH is found in Hebrews 11:1, *"Faith is the SUBSTANCE of things hoped for, the EVIDENCE of things not seen."* You will read about my early morning waking dream and how God used that dream to move me out of bed and start walking in the upcoming devotional *The Emotional Will of God*. Months before that dream, I meditated on His healing promises and looked at that varsity football picture that reminded me of running. In the same way that God supernaturally healed Dodie of liver cancer, He supernaturally healed my leg so I could walk again. There are ways God works to bring about healing, and in the following section, I will outline a few of the steps I followed.

6 PRINCIPLES OF HEALING

"What you become pregnant with in your inward spirit will produce in your outward circumstance when mixed with faith." ~Scott Hogle

Early in my cancer journey, I asked God daily, "What do you want me to do today?" God gave me specific life-saving strategies to follow. Some steps were spiritual, and some were practical, which He gave me over time. It's important that you seek God for a sure word and direction for your situation. Following are some steps God gave me as I walked out my healing journey.

1. **GET INTO FAITH:** There is a difference between having faith and being in faith. You can believe God can move mountains, but do you believe He can move a mountain through you? I needed to be in faith for my healing, not just *believe* that God can heal. The best way to get IN FAITH is to get a word from God about your situation and then meditate on it. As you read and ruminate on what God is saying to you about your situation, His Word, like a seed, will become pregnant in your spirit. What becomes pregnant in your spirit will

come out in your circumstance when you water it. How do you water it? The seed of faith grows by meditating on it and thinking about it. Getting in faith is simply planting God's living and active Word in your spirit and then watering it with meditation. The more you water it, the more it grows.

2. **GET A PICTURE AND A PROMISE FOR YOUR SITUATION:** There are over 8,000 promises in the Bible. When I struggle with something, I ask myself, "Who can I read about in the Bible that went through something similar; how did God handle their situation?" As I read their story, God speaks to me about *my* story. How do you know when God is giving you a promise from the Bible? When a verse starts to resonate inside of you, it is resonating for a reason. When it impacts you, God is imparting it to you. Here are a few Scriptures that became alive and active to me in my season of healing.

"By His stripes I am healed; I have heard your prayers and seen your tears, I will heal you says the Lord; You sent your word to heal them" (Ref. Isaiah 53:5, 2 Kings 20:4, Psalms 107:20). As I read these, they impacted me. So I read, reread, and reread them again until I was able to push out all doubt and unbelief.

Circumstances scream very loud, especially when they come with pain, a picture, or a doctor's report. Pain is a constant reminder of what's happening in the natural. It is when your body is screaming at you the loudest that you need God's promises to hang on to. I can't tell you how many times I had to renew my mind to intentionally put God's Word above my circumstances or the doctor's report, but it was a lot. I wasn't living in denial; I had the doctor's report, the PET scans, and the blood test results. There was no question in the natural about the evidence. But I was walking by faith, not by sight, and while I did, I was using the **pictures and scriptures** God led me to in order to change my internal image and talk track. The weapons we use, the Word of God, are mighty for pulling down strongholds, doubt, and unbelief within us.

3. **REFILL YOUR FAITH TANK DAILY TO STAY IN FAITH:** You leak, I leak, we all leak faith. Faith comes by hearing the Word of God and we need to keep hearing scripture that builds our faith so we can stay full. By reciting Scriptures of promise specific to my situation, I was strengthened, and my confidence in God grew. In the book of Daniel, Daniel said, "He spoke and I was strengthened." When you are contending with a doctor's report, MRIs, X-rays, PET scans, or a body that is screaming at you, you will need to refill your faith tank daily. On one occasion, God said to me, "Build yourself up on your most holy faith." I knew this meant to pray in the spirit, and I did as often as I was able. Using the spiritual weapons of worship and the Word will keep your faith meter full.

4. **GET A DAILY INSTRUCTION:** Each morning, I would ask God, "What do you want me to do today?" Some people get answers that have to do with changing their diets or lifestyle, while others get prescribed other things by the Lord. You need practical and

spiritual instruction from the Lord when you are in crisis. It is true not just for a medical situation but also for relational, financial, vocational, and other issues. I remember a time when God said to me, "Don't be double-minded." It was His way of telling me to resist fear, doubt, and anyone who would suggest anything contrary to what He was saying about my situation. That was His instruction for that day *and* all the days following. You see, my biggest battle was with myself and resisting the temptation to think the worst or worry about tomorrow. Another time, God told me to go get prayer from my Pastor, John Tilton, as a way of following Biblical protocol for healing outlined in James 5:14-15. God would use a combination of Western medicine, practical steps, faith steps, and other strategies to bring about my healing. I learned there is no bad way to get healed, but there is a God way. God's way is to get His instructions and follow them.

> *"I wanted an instantaneous healing which is a miracle. But God's way for me was to receive a healing miracle that unfolded over time."*

5. **GET INTO AGREEMENT:** The Bible says that one can put a thousand to flight, but two can put ten thousand. This is God-math at its best. If God can make a sidewalk through the Red Sea, healing your disease is no big deal for Him. But there are specific spiritual tools, principles, and laws that He puts to work. I've mentioned some of them already; another is the LAW OF

AGREEMENT, which is critical to receiving a miracle. Jesus said that where two or more are praying in His name, He is there in the midst of them, and a cord of three is not easily broken. Praying in agreement brings a force multiplier into the equation. In my season of seeking healing, I gravitated toward those who came into agreement with me for healing and avoided those who were filled with fear. When you come into agreement with a spirit-filled Christian, your prayers take flight. One of my favorite promises is found in Jeremiah 1:12, *"I look after My word to perform it."*

6. **GUARD YOUR HEART AND CONFESSION:** James 1:5-8 reveals a spiritual law I refer to as The Law of Faith: If you pray in faith but walk in doubt, your prayer request will not be granted. The Apostle James goes as far as to say that if we allow doubt to mix with our faith, we are double-minded. That may sound harsh, but I took it as a warning to guard my heart (what I let in) and watch my confession (what I allow out of my mouth). Jesus said in Matthew 12:34, *"From the depths of the heart, the mouth speaks."* This means that my words reveal what is in my heart. For this reason, when I was in danger of violating the Law of Faith (my faith was weakening or wavering), I guarded my heart and mouth so I would not disqualify myself from receiving from God. It's sad to say, but many Christians pray in faith, then walk out of prayer and speak in doubt. Their doubt counter-balances their faith to prevent the power of God from flowing. They say they believe God can do it but doubt God will do it

for or through them. When my life and cancer-eaten leg were at stake, I guarded my heart to stay in faith and protected my confession by watching the words that came out of my mouth. Here are specific directions the Apostle James gave:

> *"But if any of you lacks wisdom, let him ask of God, who gives to all generously and without reproach, and it will be given to him. But he must ask in faith without any doubting, for the one who doubts is like the surf of the sea, driven and tossed by the wind. For that person ought not to expect that he will receive anything from the Lord, being a double-minded man, unstable in all his ways."* James 1:5-8

When you pray for a miracle, guard your heart and confession so you do not disqualify yourself from receiving from God.

REFLECT TO CONNECT

1. Do you have a circumstance screaming at you right now? What does God's word say about it?
2. Have you ever considered Googling Bible verses about what you are struggling with to help you build up an arsenal of Scriptures that build your faith?
3. Do you attend a church where they believe in healing and miracles? If not, where could you look to find one?

Got Fear?

"For God hath not given us the spirit of fear; but of power, and of love, and of a sound mind" 2 Timothy 1:7 (KJV).

While at one of my son's high school baseball games, he was in the batter's box when a 70-mile-an-hour fastball came at him. Instead of going over the plate, it hit him in the side. I could hear the thud from where I sat. After the game, I asked him if he was OK, and he said, "Sure, I knew it was gonna hit me."

"How did you know?"

Bailey replied," I read it off the pitcher's fingertips." I asked him why he didn't get out of the way, and he answered, "If I wear it, I will get on base."

"Wearing it" means, "When they throw inside, don't move out of the way." Baseball players know that winning games is about hits, not runs. To win in baseball and in life, you may have to learn to "wear" those fastballs that come at you. Learning to retrain your brain to persevere through short-term pain is the first step to embracing God's way of repurposing pain for eternal purposes.

You can train yourself to neutralize your fears. Fear is a learned emotion. If it can be learned, it can be unlearned. As a child, there were probably many things you were afraid of. Are you still fearful of the same things today? Maybe some of them, but most childhood fears resolve as we grow up. We mature, gain new knowledge, and can distinguish between real fears and those in our imagination. Fear can be conquered. If you don't overcome it, you will be overcome by it. In his bestselling book *How to Master the Art of Selling*, Tom Hopkins says, "Do what you fear most, and you control fear." The opposite is true, too. The Apostle Peter said it this way, *"For by what anyone is overcome, by this he is enslaved"* (2 Peter 2:19).

RETRAIN YOUR BRAIN TO REFRAME YOUR FEAR

"Learn to do well." Isaiah 1:17

Mid-Pacific has one of the longest-standing and most successful baseball programs in Hawaii. Their training regimen and commitment to Kaizen are legendary. Kaizen is the process of continual improvement. One of their training methods for catchers is to have them put on their equipment but not give them a catcher's mitt. A player or coach then pitches a fastball that hits the ground right in front of them, so it bounces up and hits their body. The successful catcher has to learn to block the ball with their body. This serves two purposes. It teaches the catchers to use their bodies to block the ball, and it RETRAINS THEIR BRAIN so that they are not afraid of a fastball. It's counter-intuitive to run toward your fears, but you will discover that as you do, most of them are neutralized. The closer you can get to your fears, the smaller they become. Why? Because fear is like a roaring lion without teeth. It can be overcome and neutralized. So, what are you afraid of? A conversation, a confrontation, maybe a relationship? Like the batter in the batting box getting ready to wear a fastball so they can advance to their base, what fastball do you need to wear so God can advance you to your next season in life? Wear it and watch to see what He does.

"Don't let the circumstances you face become bigger than the God you are following." ~Scott Hogle

F.E.A.R. will sabotage your destiny if you don't learn to deal with it. F.E.A.R. can stop you from having important conversations, asking for a raise, confronting bad behavior, picking up the phone, taking a trip, and the list goes on. The ten spies scouting the promise land let fear sabotage their destiny. They put what they saw above what God said. Making their circumstances bigger than their God caused them to fall into fear. Fear is Satan's #1 tool for self-sabotage. If he can capture your attention, he can direct your thoughts and emotions. Your life will follow the direction of your most dominant thoughts and feelings. You must master fear, or fear will master you. Fear is not a one-time set-it-and-forget-it thing; you must manage it throughout your lifetime. Fear is not of God but it is part of the old nature. For adults, fear masks itself in the form of apprehension, anxiety, denial, and stress. Fear is a relentless predator, always hunting to capture its prey and hold it hostage. Once you break free from the cage of fear, it will relentlessly pursue you, trying to recapture and enslave you once more.

In 1 Peter 5:8, scripture tells us that your adversary "Prowls like a roaring lion, seeking someone to devour." Satan's tactic is designed to make you capitulate and surrender to the fear.

Just as some predators in the wild can smell fear, so too can the demonic. God has given us FIGHT VS. FLIGHT instincts for a reason, to protect us. When we feel threatened, we will either choose to stand and fight or turn and run. F.E.A.R. can stand for "Face Everything and Rise" or "Forget Everything and Run."

In most cases, our fears never come true—they are false. I like the F.E.A.R. acronym, which stands for False Evidence Appearing Real. Whether the threat is real or not, if the enemy can make you believe you are in danger, that belief alone is enough to enslave you through fear.

> *"No weapon that is formed against you will succeed; And you will condemn every tongue that accuses you in judgment. This is the heritage of the servants of the LORD, And their vindication is from Me"* Isaiah. 54:17

WORRY IS MEDITATING ON F.E.A.R.

Are you addicted to F.E.A.R.? I certainly was at one time. Fears that I overcame in my 20s were replaced by new fears in my 30s. Early in my career, I had what I call "A great fear of failure." I grew up in middle America, where we didn't have much, and money was always a struggle. Once I tasted success and didn't have to worry about living month-to-month anymore, it was the fear of losing it all that drove me to press in and work around the clock. Fear is a powerful, motivating emotion. But what starts as motivation can turn into a drive that feels unstoppable and has serious consequences. Chronic fear has serious negative effects on your body. It continually spikes your adrenaline and cortisol, raises your blood pressure and heart rate, and blood flows away from the heart and into your limbs. This is the opposite of God's design, providing a life-giving energy through a life of faith.

When Covid hit in 2020, F.E.A.R. paralyzed the world overnight. There were times when I found myself swept up into it. The early protocols of wearing masks and sheltering in place quickly became a runaway freight train that fed a spirit of fear, seemingly taking over the country. Fear paralyzed our communities and crippled our churches. As I talked to God, He dropped this statement into my heart, "America's #1 addiction is fear." If you watch the news, it is filled with worry about what might happen, but it rarely does. The goal of national cable news is not to report the news but to sensationalize news to keep you tuned in so ratings remain high. It promotes and plays on your fears, effectively keeping you tuned in. The goal of F.E.A.R. is to get you to worry. Instead of getting you to set your mind on THINGS ABOVE, the enemy wants you to worry and mediate on your fears and have them become the dominant thoughts in your life. If you are addicted to fear, you are standing in agreement with the enemy. There can be no agreement between faith and fear simultaneously. And we know that "Without faith, it is impossible to please God."

3 STRATEGIES FOR CONQUERING F.E.A.R.

"We have nothing to fear except fear itself."
~Franklin D. Roosevelt

I refuse to live in fear and will NOT be held hostage by my fears or insecurities. I have discovered that as I run toward my fears, they do get smaller. As I embrace my fear, they lose their grip. When I do what I fear most, I neutralize fear. If you are experiencing a sort of emotional apprehension about doing or saying something, then F.E.A.R. may have a grip on you. Whatever you are fearing, DO IT ANYWAYS, and set yourself free. Here are a few strategies I use to confront and conquer my fear:

1. **NEUTRALIZE YOUR FEAR WITH A GOD PROMISE.** There are over 8000 promises in the Bible. When you are faced with a fear, find one of the promises that relates to your situation. Meditate on it, recite it, and remind yourself and others of it often. This will allow God's promise to become the most dominant thought surrounding your circumstance. I was once asked to speak after recovering from a season when I had lost my voice. I didn't know if my voice box would hold up, as it was recovering from radiation treatment, but I said yes anyway. In the two weeks leading up to the day I was asked to speak, I meditated on and recited in my heart, over and over again, *"I can do all things through Christ who strengthens me; In my weakness, your power is made perfect; No weapon formed against me shall prosper."* When you say what God has said, you feel what God feels toward you. I was able to MIND-SHIFT my thoughts using the Word of God, and in so doing, switched my emotions from the fear of what might happen to faith in what God could do. *In the face of God's power, my fears were neutralized.* Our emotions result from our thinking, which is a way of saying our feelings are created by what we are meditating on. The Apostle

Paul advised us to *"THINK ON THESE THINGS"* in chapter 4 of Philippians. Paul knew that there is a correlation between what we think about and what we feel. God promised in Isaiah 26:3, *"You will keep them in perfect peace, whose mind is stayed on you."* What you think about grows inside of you. It's time you start to think about what you are thinking about.

2. **BEN FRANKLIN YOUR FACTS AND FEELINGS!**
Have you ever heard the expression, "Don't confuse me with the facts; I've made up my mind"? That sounds ridiculous, but it is how some people behave. Why? Because fear causes people to think, say, and do irrational things. Fear creates confusion; it makes us unreasonable. It can sabotage your future and corrupt your present. Each of us has a fear and faith nature within us. You will need to learn how to talk to yourself about your situation, or your self-talk will do all the talking. In my mind's eye, I envision a traffic cop at the entrance of my mind that helps to sift through the real vs. the imagined thoughts. It is what is meant by *"Take every thought captive to the obedience of Christ."* Some thoughts you simply cannot entertain, because once you do, you fall prey to them, and the emotions surrounding them can overwhelm you. Sometimes, you have to tell yourself to shut up. To help me separate facts from feelings, I

use the Ben Franklin method. I draw a line down the center of a piece of paper, listing the facts on one side and the feelings on the other. This helps me objectively separate the two. I also use this method to renew my mind by writing down my "self-talk thoughts" on one side and what God's Word says about the same thing on the other side. This process allows me to use Jesus's strategy of combatting the enemy's thoughts by responding with "IT IS WRITTEN." Help God speak to you by outlining the facts, your feelings, what you are thinking, and what His Word says on paper. This is a powerful method to help you overcome, as God often uses journaling to confirm through the pen what the Spirit has spoken.

3. **TURN UP YOUR FAITH TO TURN DOWN YOUR FEAR.** Feelings are like a volume button. You can turn them from a loud roar to a whisper or even turn them from on to off. How do you gain control over fear? By putting your faith above your feelings. The first time I received the doctor's report saying I had cancer, I remember exactly where I was sitting. I consulted with God before trusting what I felt. God spoke to my heart and said, "Whose report are you going to believe?" I remember thinking at the time, "What an odd thing to ask me, Lord; the doctor's report is in my hand." What God was really saying to me was that he wanted me to trust in Him and not in the doctor's report. From that day on, I read up on what the Bible says about healing and meditated on that, not on what the report or the

internet had to say. Don't let the circumstances you face become bigger than the God you are following.

REFLECT TO CONNECT

1. As you outline your dominant thoughts and feelings on paper, what are they saying to you?
2. What obstacles have you faced where you overcame your fears with the truth of God's word?
3. Can you recall when you trusted what your eyes saw more than what God's Word promised?

The Herald in Heaven

"… So that the manifold wisdom of God might now be made known through the church to the rulers and the authorities in the heavenly places." Ephesians 3:10

In the nineteenth century, paper boys would stand on the corner holding up the morning edition of the newspaper and yell, "Read all about it!" They were known as heralds who proclaimed the headlines of the day. Reporters for the newspaper are scribes who write about news and events worthy of printing in the daily newspaper. I grew up in Chicago, and as a young boy, I delivered the Chicago Tribune. Rain or shine, snow or sun, I was up at the crack of dawn rolling papers and securing them with rubber bands. Then, I'd load them into the baskets of my Schwinn and head out to deliver the morning news. As early as it was, there would be people waiting for their papers and eager to read the headline of the day.

In the same way, the testimony of your life "makes news" to those in the heavenly realm every day. It is through your life being lived in Christ that God's glory is made manifest. In the Book of Daniel, we learn about the Watchers—angels who carry out God's commands and keep records. In Acts 10:1, Cornelius is visited by an angel, indicating that all his prayers and charitable acts have been recorded. One day, we will stand before Christ to receive rewards for what we've done. Even now, in heaven, there is a book with your name on it—If your name is Mary, perhaps it's called the Book of Mary or the Acts of Mary. God keeps track of your service, your sacrifices, and your prayers. If God knows the number of hairs on your head, how much more does He know your thoughts and ways? Your Divine Destiny is very important to Him, and every step you take as you walk into eternity matters deeply.

YOUR LIFE IS A LIVING TESTIMONY TO THE SPIRITUAL REALM

Have you ever had the sense that someone was watching you? They are. Besides the angels who watch over you and minister to you, there is the great cloud of witnesses in the heavenly realm looking down on you, cheering you on (Hebrews 12:1). Your life serves as a herald in heaven, proclaiming the workings of God as a witness to the angels and those Christ has appointed to manage the spiritual realm. Angels long to observe how God operates in your life, as they do not experience God's redemptive power and manifold wisdom as humanity does. Your life is a living testimony.

BECOMING A HERALD IN HEAVEN

God sends you to share your story so others will be strengthened. When I was diagnosed with cancer, my wife and I decided to keep it quiet. Our sons were young, and I didn't want to share it with others. It was more my decision than hers, but nonetheless, she agreed. I would later learn that she shared my news with some ladies in her women's group.

I was quite upset and felt that she betrayed my trust. I called her on the phone, was angry, and yelled at her. She shared that she wanted people to be praying for me and that these were trustworthy women.

The minute I hung up the phone, God whispered to my heart, "I will decide who is on the prayer list." I learned many things in that season, and one of "the big ones" was that the supporting spouse is often struggling too and in need of prayer and support, sometimes more than the patient. God also showed me that my decision not to share my struggle was short-circuiting His ability to demonstrate His strength and healing power in my life. It is in my weakness and through the prayers of other people that His power is made perfect. As I shared my story, I found others were strengthened. As people heard about what God did in my life, it gave them hope for their own journey.

My journey with Christ is a herald in the heavenly and earthly realms. To this day, I am still not comfortable sharing all the intimate details of my life, but I am intentional about doing it. I may never be comfortable, but now that I understand the importance of sharing my struggles, God can use them to strengthen me and others. I am diligent in testifying so that I can cooperate with His plan. You and I were created to bring God glory. We do this by proclaiming His great works in our lives, by testifying of His grace, wisdom, and power. If we keep silent, how will people hear? If we don't step forward, who will speak up and share the greatness of God?

If you are unsure of the testimony God is building in your life, ask Him. In due season, you will have a story God wants you to share. When that time comes, herald it from the rooftops.

"You should always carry two books with you, the one you are reading and the one you are writing."
~ Kevin Hall, author of *Aspire*

REFLECT TO CONNECT

1. What struggle in your life does God want you to share as a way to strengthen others?
2. Whose testimony has helped you draw closer to God?
3. Why does sharing testimony give people hope?

The Romans 8:28 Roundtrip

"And we know that God causes all things to work together for good to those who love God, to those who are called according to His purpose" Romans 8:28.

Romans 8:28 ROUNDTRIP is when God takes you on a journey, and when you arrive, you're better off than when you started. Sometimes, this journey might feel like you're moving in circles, going backward, or taking detours, but God brings everything together for His purposes. He has a way of making things work out better in the end than they began. Sometimes you can see how God is connecting the dots, and sometimes you can't. That's why it's important to trust in the goodness of God and remember to walk by faith, not by sight. The next time you find yourself in the middle of a ROMANS 8:28 ROUNDTRIP, remember that God has a plan that requires your participation, including obedience, patience, and cooperation.

God's specialty is to use your troubles as transportation to lead you into the next season. As you walk into your Divine Destiny, the journey is not a straight line. You may find yourself in hills, valleys, zig-zags, and even ditches. God uses the difficulty in the terrain to build your spiritual muscles and grow you into the full measure of Christ. Like with Daniel's three friends, He uses the heat in the furnace of testing to reshape and remake you into a vessel fit for the Master's use. Sometimes, God will use fire or famine to motivate you along on the next leg of your Romans 8:28 Roundtrip. God used a famine to bring Jacob to Egypt, positioning him for the future He had planned for Israel through a man named Moses.

Similarly, God used a dried-up brook to motivate Elijah to MOVE from where he was to where God wanted him to be. God uses famines and challenges to move us from one place to another, aligning us with His greater plans. Sometimes it's about us, and sometimes it's not. You may be experiencing a famine in love and dealing with loneliness or a job-related famine, but whatever "famine" you are in, God's going to open a door. There are also famines of direction, making you feel like a ship without a rudder. Know that God has a purpose in this, too, and is about to reveal it to you.

GOD USES FAMINE TO MOTIVATE AND MOVE YOU

"God's specialty is to use your troubles as transportation, to lead you into the next season." ~Scott Hogle

Where is the famine, the lack, or the scarcity in your life right now? Early in my career, I experienced a great run of success. I was well-liked and well-paid. Success seemed to be around every corner… until it wasn't. What happened? What went wrong? The company I worked for was sold. I went from having great favor and finances to a famine in both. I noticed the new team didn't look at me like the old team did. They didn't value me as my former manager had. I was experiencing a famine in favor. Then, they changed my job, causing me to experience a famine in finances. My pain ratcheted up over the months, and I started asking God, "What's going on? What are you doing?" God uses pain to get our attention. Instead of asking God "why," which is a question to nowhere, I learned over the years to ask the Lord, "How do you want to use this?" God can work with "how," but He will not always answer the "why." While the Waymaker is working things behind the scenes, He needs you to stay in faith because He can't reveal His strategy in the middle of your Romans 8:28 Roundtrip. The teacher is always silent while the test is going on. God used a famine in favor and finances to MOVE me from one place to another. I didn't want to go, but my circumstances forced me to seek out a new job. There were three things I learned in that season that I have carried with me, and they have served me well.

3 LIFE LESSONS ON THE ROMANS 8:28 ROUNDTRIP

1. DIVINE MENTORSHIP: My losses can be leveraged for my benefit if I give them to God. God will turn my losses into lessons IF I bring them to Him. The word "IF" appears in the Bible over 300 times. Some of God's blessings and promises are conditional on your participation. God will NOT override you if you resist Him. He will wait until you are ready to surrender. When struggling, sometimes I make mistakes, and I may not be thinking properly, but God can use that too. It's one of the wonders of how the Waymaker works. He not only turned my losses into lessons, but He then

LEVERAGED them to take me to higher ground; it's part of the Romans 8:28 Roundtrip journey. He puts my feet upon a rock and gives me a new story in the season. What testimony is God building in your life? Is it possible that what He is building will become a bridge to transport you to your next season?

"Just because you are struggling doesn't mean you are failing." ~John Maxwell, bestselling author

2. HEALTHY RELATIONSHIPS: The second thing I learned is to go where I am celebrated, not just tolerated. Not everyone in your life will see your value. When you experience a famine in favor, that's a divine clue that God is preparing to move you into a new season, a new place, and with a new group of people. Jesus told the 70 to let their peace remain where they were welcomed, but if they were rejected, to let their peace return to them and depart. If you are facing rejection and are not being received, it's moving day. Get ready for a shift! Part of your Romans 8:28 Roundtrip may require traveling and leaving some people and places behind. Is there a relationship God is asking you to let go of in preparation for a new person He wants to bring you?

"God talks to us in our conscience, whispers to us in our pleasure, but shouts at us in our pain." ~C.S. Lewis

3. LOOSENING ROOTS: The third thing I learned is that when God is relocating me, He is repositioning me to

be in alignment with Him for my Divine Destiny. As He readies me for transition, He will allow earthquakes and famine to <u>loosen up my root system in the place I am planted</u>. I am referring to challenging circumstances. If God tried to move me without an earthquake in my circumstance, the rapid ejection could damage my faith or worse… I could refuse to be moved because things are going so well. But when the ground starts to shake under my feet and my circumstances become difficult, my deep root system starts to loosen. I've seen this many times in my life when the tectonic plates begin to shake or shift; it leads me to look up and ask God, "What are you doing? Are you giving me a heads up on something about to happen?" When God repositions, He repositions for a purpose that usually involves some pain. Is there a pain point God is using to loosen your root system where you are currently planted?

REFLECT TO CONNECT

1. Why is it important to ask God "how" He wants to use something vs. "why" is this happening to me?
2. What Romans 8:28 ROUNDTRIP has God brought you through where you finished better than you started?
3. What earthquake or circumstance of famine have you walked through? What advice would you give to a friend facing the same?

The Dual Assignment

"And Jesus said, 'Occupy until I come back'" Luke 19:13.

Over 85% of Jesus's messages had a workplace context and were given in the marketplace, not the synagogue. That means that almost nine out of ten people He was talking to were called to live out their faith in their everyday careers, not the ministry. That doesn't mean you don't also have an assignment in the ministry. In fact, the Apostle Peter affirms this when He refers to you as a king and priest. *"But you are **a chosen people,** A **royal priesthood, a holy nation, a people for God's own possession,** so that you may proclaim the excellencies of Him who has called you out of darkness into His marvelous light,"* 1 Peter 2:9. That means you walk in a priestly and kingly anointing wherever you are. You carry this dual anointing everywhere. You are a king and priest in your home, church, work, and your community.

THE IMPARTATION

"Do not leave Jerusalem, but wait for the gift My Father promised, which you have heard Me speak about. But you will receive power when the Holy Spirit comes on you, and you will be My witnesses." Acts 1:4, 8

How is your natural talent different from the supernatural gifts given by God? Your natural talents were given to you while you were yet being formed in your mother's womb (Jeremiah 1:5). God decided your talents before birth; it is up to you to discover and develop them. God gives a part of Himself to every person, which is a unique set of gifts that make up your gift matrix. You have God's DNA within you; you were created in His image (Genesis 1:26). Supernatural gifts are given to serve in both your marketplace and ministry assignments. Discovering your gifts helps you identify your short- and long-term assignments, as gifting is linked to your calling. God provides the necessary talents and gifts for each assignment, many of which may be unlocked at just the right time. This means God might unlock a gift for you in your 40s that you didn't have in your 20s or release an anointing and assignment that lay dormant in your 40s until you reach your 60s. Just as the Jordan River did not part until the priest put their feet in it, your gifts may not be unlocked until your feet enter the path of your Divine Destiny. Natural giftings will get you *onto* the road of your Divine Destiny, and spiritual giftings will empower you to *complete* your Divine Destiny. In the MANA devotional, I discuss how God can anoint your natural talents to produce a supernatural result.

WITHIN YOU VS. UPON YOU

What is the difference between the Holy Spirit living in you vs. being activated within you? You can receive a supernatural impartation through prayer, the laying on of hands, or by exercising your gifts. Yet the anointing may remain dormant and not manifest unless you put it to work. Why is this? Because the gift of the prophet is subject *to* the prophet (Romans 12:6). A gift may naturally unfold over time as you work in your assignment, but the anointing sometimes needs to be stirred into service. The Holy Spirit lives inside of you, and He likes to be stirred (2 Timothy 1:6); said another way, He likes to be put to work in marketplace and ministry situations *with you*. This is the DRAWING OUT of the anointing within you, and you can do it at your own pace according to your measure of faith.

There is another type of impartation that is even more powerful than when you stir the anointing within you. It is when the Holy Spirit comes UPON YOU. When the Holy Spirit came upon Saul to make him king, the Scripture says he "became another man." The Apostle Peter was in fear, hiding out, and denied Jesus three times. But when the Holy Spirit came UPON him, he spoke with boldness about Christ, and thousands were saved. In Old Testament times, the Holy Spirit would come upon Samson and give him super-strength to carry out the work God had given him to do. Elijah supernaturally outran a chariot, and the Holy Spirit came UPON Philip, which empowered him to run with super-speed to catch up to a chariot so he could witness to an Ethiopian. A young shepherd boy named David took a sheep from a lion and bear, and the anointing gave his sling super speed and accuracy to kill the giant named Goliath.

These are examples of the Holy Spirit coming UPON someone to create supernatural feats of strength, speed, and boldness. There is no limit to the gifts or manifestations the Holy Spirit working within and upon you can have. His power and the work He has for your Divine Destiny will be specific to you. Your dual assignment comes with a dual anointing for the marketplace and ministry. As you move in your lane of calling and draw upon the supply of the Spirit, you will experience the stirring within and upon.

REFLECT TO CONNECT

1. When have you experienced the stirring of the Holy Spirit?
2. How would you differentiate your spiritual gifts from your natural gifts? Have you identified them?
3. When have you experienced the power and anointing of God?

Anointed for the Assignment

PART I

"Now concerning spiritual gifts, brothers and sisters, I do not want you to be unaware; Now there are varieties of gifts, but the same Spirit. And there are varieties of ministries, and the same Lord. There are varieties of effects, but the same God who works all things in all persons. But to each one is given the manifestation of the Spirit for the common good" 1 Corinthians 12:1, 4-7.

Your dual assignment—both in the marketplace and ministry—comes with a dual anointing for both callings. God's spiritual gifts aren't confined to just one area of your life. If your gift operates in one area, it will also function in the other. For example, if you have the gift of discernment and wisdom in your marketplace role, it will carry over into your ministry role as well. Similarly, if you receive words of knowledge at church, you can also receive them in your work life.

GIFT CLUSTERS

"Not by might, nor by power, but by my spirit, saith the LORD of hosts." Ref. Zechariah 4:6

"Have you tasted of the heavenly gift and been made a partaker of powers of the age to come?" (Hebrews 6:5) Of the spiritual gifts mentioned in the Bible, some work in cooperation. For example, when the Word of Wisdom is in operation, the Word of Knowledge and the Spirit of Discernment are also present. When the gift of prophecy is in operation, so may the gift of tongues and the interpretation of tongues. In the same way, the gift of faith, miracles, and healing may go hand in hand. Those with the gift of giving may also move in a gift of help or mercy. Do you know what cluster of gifts the Holy Spirit desires to impart to you? I have asked God before, "I'm on assignment here; can you please provide some favor?" and favor shows up. I've requested, "I need your help; please show me what I don't see," and God gives me discernment. When I am stuck, I ask, "What am I supposed to do?" and I get an idea in the form of a Word of Wisdom or Knowledge. What are you struggling with? What has God called you to in this season of your life? You have access to ALL spiritual blessings and giftings necessary for the work ahead. Below are a few practical examples of how spiritual gifts can function in your life. Understanding how spiritual gifts practically function in everyday life is essential to reaching your Divine Destiny.

THE WORD OF KNOWLEDGE & WISDOM

*"A Word of Knowledge is knowing 'what to do,'
the gift of wisdom is knowing 'how or when to do it.'"*

I was in a business meeting with someone from Enterprise Rental Car for about an hour, and just when I thought the meeting was about to end, he started asking me about the church I go to. Then he asked about my service there, my educational background, and so on. Fifteen minutes went by, and he kept asking me questions about myself and my story. That's when God spoke to me and said, "Scott, he's not asking about you. He's asking about me." This was a supernatural <u>Word of Knowledge</u>. I stopped the conversation and asked him if he had ever accepted Christ as his personal Lord and Savior. He said, "No." The Lord then told me NOT to offer to pray with him just yet, but to explain the importance of forgiveness, grace, sin, and why Jesus came and died for our sins. At the end of the conversation, I asked him if he wanted to accept Christ, and he said "yes," so we prayed.

A Word of Knowledge is knowing *what to do*; the Gift of Wisdom is *knowing how or when to do it*. God showed me *what* to do and then *how to* do it. Whenever I am struggling and need a solution to a business or relationship problem, I lean on James 1:5, which says, "But if any of you lacks wisdom, let him ask of God, who gives to all generously and without reproach, and it will be given to him." Here is a secret to receiving a Word of Knowledge or Wisdom. Before you pray, get yourself into a neutral state, letting go of any insistence on a specific answer from God. Allow Him to answer as He wills. Then, get quiet before God and ask your question.

As you wait in peace, pay attention to what comes to mind and write down what you hear, receiving it by faith. Pray about your answer, and when you feel peace or receive confirmation, take action and put God's answer to work; He will do the rest. I regularly write out my questions and challenges to God on paper. I also pray them out loud in the Spirit, expecting an answer. I noticed that the more I expect, the more I get.

Nonetheless, God answers in His time, not mine. Is there something you need a supernatural insight or strategy for? This is what the Word of Knowledge and Wisdom are for. God delights in giving generously to all who seek Him.

GIFT OF DISCERNMENT

"Like apples of gold in settings of silver Is a word spoken in right circumstances."
Proverbs 25:11

The gift of discernment is the ability to read a situation, an environment, or a person. It goes beyond emotional intelligence; it is <u>God-inspired spiritual intelligence</u> at work in you to supernaturally pull the curtain back, revealing emotion, motive, and intent. Jesus said in Matthew 15:8, *"These people honor me with their lips, but their hearts are far from me."* When Jesus said this, He was exercising the Gift of Discernment. Their words and body language said one thing, but their hearts were hiding a different message. Have you ever sensed this while talking with someone?

On one occasion, during a business call, I received some surprising news from a supervisor that shocked me. The information I received was so out of character for my company and how they normally handled this type of situation that I was caught off guard and didn't know what to say. I had a strong sense that I should end the call and call a trusted advisor whom God had put on my heart. That strong sense was the Spirit of Discernment, a Word of instruction from God. I ended the call and called the person God put on my heart. I shared my situation and asked them to speak to it. I encouraged them to say the first thing that came to their mind and said, "I believe God is going to speak to me through you." I immediately rejected the insight he gave me. *"But the natural man does not receive the things of the Spirit of God, for they are foolishness to him; nor can he know them because they are spiritually discerned"*(1 Corinthians 2:14). But the Holy Spirit bore witness in my spirit that what he just told me was accurate. I KNEW in my KNOWER that what he told me was true. What happened? My *natural mind* rejected what God was saying, but my spirit discerned that it was accurate. The gift of discernment was at work. Months later, the very thing my trusted advisor communicated to me, which I first rejected that the Spirit then confirmed, was also confirmed by someone else in my company. Having the Gift of Discernment both in your personal life and at work will help you to read a situation and read people and know what to do. Next time your spiritual senses (intuition) start to tingle about a situation, may I suggest you pause, get quiet, and ask God to give you a Spirit of Discernment?

*"Trust in the LORD with all your heart and do not lean on
your own understanding. In all your ways acknowledge Him,
And He will make your paths straight."*
Proverbs 3:5-6

"And it shall be in the last days, saith God, I will pour forth of my Spirit upon all flesh: And your sons and your daughters shall prophesy, And your young men shall see visions, And your old men shall dream dreams." Acts 2:17

Have you ever woken up from sleep after having a vivid dream? It was as if you had just seen a movie play out across the screen of your mind. A dream can come with great detail but also divine instruction. Joseph had the gift of dreams and the interpretation of dreams. God would use Joseph's gift to promote him, then provide a blueprint for navigating a future famine so Egypt and Israel would be provided for. The Apostle Paul dreamed of a man in Macedonia waving to him and asking for help. He concluded that the dream was from the Holy Spirit and that He was directing his steps; Paul was right. If a dream is from God, you will have a witness in your heart, a strong sense of rightness for a thing. In 2011, God gave my friend Steve Sombrero a dream with a math equation in it. That dream would remain pregnant in Steve's heart for years. A decade later, God would turn a math equation into a REVELATION, which would birth a VISION for Steve to publish a book. Steve's book *What Day Are You?* gave him a platform to share his testimony about the day he tried to commit suicide and how God intervened with a Christian song playing on the radio to give him hope. Steve's book and story are a messenger of hope for people who have become hopeless. Have you had a dream where you KNEW God was trying to get a message to you? Maybe God is giving you a heads up of something coming that contains a blueprint like He did

Joseph. Or maybe God gave you an idea hidden in a piece of information that is unfolding over time like He did Steve. Is there a dream you have received that you can't shake? When you have a dream, write it down so you can place it before the Lord and pray about it. If it's from God, desire will rise within you to take action, and providential doors will open before you. If it is not from God, the dream will fade over time. The Gift of Dreams and their interpretation can be an important piece of your Divine Destiny.

GIFT OF FAITH

T.J., who you read about on Day One, was called to Christian Broadcasting. I refer to him as a broadcast apostle because he has taken the gospel to unreached places using broadcast media. He worked for CBN in the early 1990s when the Berlin Wall fell. He was a trailblazer, bringing Christian broadcasting into communist countries for the first time. God gifted him with supernatural faith, enabling him to cross borders and enter dangerous, war-torn areas to spread the gospel in places where it had never been before, including Israel, Lebanon, and the Soviet Union. This kind of calling requires a supernatural FAITH that empowers people to walk into danger with courageous confidence. The Gift of Faith is a special supernatural impartation that will give you the courage to do what people normally would never do. I have great faith and boldness for *my* assignment, which is not to travel to areas where the danger of getting killed for the gospel is a daily occurrence. Why? Because I have faith for my assignment, not his. God said to Joshua, *"As I was with Moses, I will be with you. Wherever you put your foot, I will give you."* You will be given the Gift of Faith for the territory God has asked you to occupy for the kingdom. I have always liked the acronym for F.A.I.T.H.

Forward   Action   Inspired   Through   Him

REFLECT TO CONNECT

1. How would you describe your God-given spiritual gifts?
2. What spiritual gift would make you more effective in your assignment?
3. The Word of Wisdom is a divine insight on *how* to do something. How have you experienced this in your lane of assignment?

Anointed for the Assignment

PART II

"Since we have gifts that differ according to the grace given to us, each of us is to use them properly; if prophecy, in proportion to one's faith; if service, in the act of serving; or the one who teaches, in the act of teaching; or the one who exhorts, in the work of exhortation; the one who gives, with generosity; the one who is in leadership, with diligence; the one who shows mercy, with cheerfulness" Romans 12:6-8.

There are many supernatural gifts in operation in the Old and New Testaments. There are also gifts inspired by the Holy Spirit that are not listed in the Bible. According to the grace given to you and in cooperation with your assignment, God may impart these gifts not listed in the Bible. On Day 2 in MANA, I mentioned a supernatural gift God gave me for wordsmithing. As a wordsmith, there are times I am writing or speaking when the Holy Spirit will INSPIRE me to say or wordsmith something in a particular way. Until these gifts revealed themselves and I started to develop them, I had not excelled in English. When I write, I notice that my writing far surpasses my natural talent or ability. The gift of wordsmithing isn't listed in the Bible. Similarly, my wife Kate has a gift for working with numbers and spreadsheets to uncover the business stories and applications in data. She doesn't necessarily like math or numbers, but God gave her a supernatural talent for this gift. Why? Because it is part of her assignment. Through the Spirit, God can supply everything you need for the path you're on. There's no limit to what the Holy Spirit can provide for whatever you face.

> *"For I know that this shall turn to my salvation through*
> *your prayer, and the supply of the Spirit of Jesus Christ."*
> Philippians 1:19

SUPERNATURAL FAVOR

> *"And Jesus kept increasing in wisdom and stature,*
> *and in favor with God and people."*
> Luke 2:52

Why is favor so important? God uses favor to go before you, creating opportunities that accelerate your assignment. There will be times, just as it was with Jesus, when your arrival will be eagerly anticipated—when you walk into a room, people instantly honor and appreciate you as if there's a halo of acceptance hovering above you. This is God's presence shining upon you, the gift of favor. Favor creates an aura of honor and expectation, making it a powerful tool for accomplishing God's work.

How do you bring the supernatural into the natural? While I serve as a teaching Pastor at New Hope Oahu, my full-time vocation is President of iHeartMedia in Honolulu, Hawaii. My days are filled with stress, excitement, demands, and the need for miracles. Recently, my market was incorporated into a new region with new supervisors who did not know me. Overnight, my reputation, favor, and twenty-five-year track record of success were unknown to the people I now reported to. Joseph had a similar experience, as told in Exodus 1:9: *"A Pharaoh rose up who knew not Joseph."* Over the next year, opportunities to build relationship equity and trust were few and far between. I said to God, "I'm on assignment here. I need some favor." God knows what you need and does not mind you walking boldly into the Throne Room of Grace to request it. Shortly after this prayer request, my bosses came to town to visit. During a client meeting, one of our larger clients said "Yes" to my boss's presentation, doubled their spending with the company on the spot, and said, "I say yes to what Scott asks me to do." This raised my equity dramatically and my boss was able to go back to his boss with a nice win. A few days later, I called the client and thanked them for making me look so good in front of my bosses, and when I asked him why, he said, "God told me to honor you in front of your bosses." God spoke to someone on my behalf to answer my prayer! Jesus promised, *"Ask, and it shall be given."* When I asked, the answer didn't show up instantly; it took some time, but then favor materialized supernaturally.

"The king's heart is like channels of water in the hand of the LORD; He turns it wherever He pleases." Proverbs 21:1

THE CHARISMA OF CHRIST

God can impart another kind of supernatural favor to you called the Charisma of Christ. Lance Wallnau describes this as "The supernatural attraction toward you that draws people to you who are predisposed to serve you." Joseph and Daniel had this magnetic anointing in spades. The Charisma of Christ is available to you for the work you do. You can ask God for it now, anytime. As you pray with expectancy, with a heart of thanksgiving, open your eyes and look for clues of it materializing. Keep in mind that you will then need to steward the favor. If God grants you favor, but you have weak relationship skills, all the miracle power in the world will not fix what your tongue breaks. God promises to answer prayer; we must steward His answers.

THE GIFT OF GRACIOUSNESS

"Let your speech always be with grace, seasoned with salt,
that you may know how you ought to answer each one."
Colossians 4:6

The Gift of Graciousness is an "unofficial" fruit of the Spirit. My friend Gary has this gift, and whenever I see Gary, he immediately begins to thank me or speak about something he appreciates about me. As others join our conversation, he turns to them and begins to talk to them about me in a very positive light while I'm standing there. Gary will tell them of my gifts, qualities he admires, accomplishments, and so on. When he speaks highly of me to others, it lifts me up and strengthens me from within. What is Gary doing? He's using the Gift of Graciousness to cultivate an atmosphere of honor. As you develop the art of honoring others, they'll be naturally drawn to you and inclined to support you. Why? Because when people feel valued, uplifted, and elevated in your presence, it deepens your influence with them. This is one of the divine ways to grow your impact—just as Paul used the Gift of Graciousness when opening his letters to the churches.

THE GIFT OF INFLUENCE

"Therefore, encourage one another and build one another up,
just as you also are doing."
1 Thessalonians 5:11

The Gift of Gracious Communication creates influence. It can advance the gospel and demonstrate the kindness of Christ. It's a Gift of Communication that opens doors, makes a way where there is no way, and paves the way for God to work through you. The ability to create an atmosphere of grace, honor, and appreciation was evident in the style of communication the Apostle Paul used in his letters to the churches. As you read his writing, his pattern is evident, one you can emulate. The way in which Paul handles his audiences, always looking for and pointing to the best in others, creates charisma and influence for his mission. His style of communication seeks to edify and add value, always looking to build up others so they are elevated in his presence. As he does this, his influence greatly expands, and he becomes magnetic, drawing people to himself. He then points them to Christ. The Gift of Graciousness assumes the best, looks for the best, and speaks to the greatness in people, and this manifests into the Gift of Influence. The more you honor people for their gifts, contributions, and the special qualities you see in them, the more your influence and charisma grow.

"Graciousness in communication attracts gentleness in others; it draws out the greatness in people by drawing attention to God's giftings in them." ~Scott Hogle

GIFT OF ENCOURAGEMENT

Cass Langton worked for Hillsong in Australia for twenty years and once visited New Hope, Oahu. While speaking at our services, she paused and spoke out a Word of Encouragement to a number of people in the audience. How can you know if God has given you the Gift of Encouragement? God will cause you to see, feel, or sense what He's feeling or wants to say to a person, even see yourself speaking to them a specific word, praying for them, or laying hands on them. God can also give you a picture to show you what He wants you to see. Jesus once said, "I can only do what I see the Father doing." There may be times when God wants you to lay hands on someone to release healing in them. If you are in a situation and all of a sudden you <u>see yourself</u> doing something, God is prompting you to act. Your step of faith will release the power of God to flow through you to another person. This is God's heart imprinting upon your heart so you see and feel as He does. Jesus often felt compassion for someone and was "moved" to heal them. As God's heart came upon Jesus, so God's heart will come upon you when He wants to move you to use your spiritual gift. Courageously step out and trust God to do the rest. He is using you to RELEASE an impartation to someone in your world.

ENTER GOD'S SPIRITUAL WI-FI ZONE

Many spiritual gifts work in cooperation with one another. As you exercise one, another gets activated. The Holy Spirit won't stop working through you unless you resist His promptings. Like entering a Holy Spirit Wi-Fi Zone, you will know what to say, almost as if you had a headset on listening to what God wants you to do. When you receive this kind of download—a flow of insight and instruction—God is activating a gift within you to serve others and glorify Him. Get excited! There's no limit to the anointing of the Holy Spirit in your life. Through the Supply of the Spirit, you can do all things through Christ who strengthens you. If this is your first time stirring the gifts inside of you or asking the Giver of Gifts for a special impartation for your assignment, remember to give God time to work. He will work with you according to your faith. Sometimes, it takes time to receive and then develop spiritual gifts. What spiritual gift would you like to ask God for today?

REFLECT TO CONNECT

1. What steps could you take to develop the Gift of Graciousness?
2. What could you use the Charisma of Christ to accomplish?
3. What God-given gifts have you experienced that are not listed in the Bible?

Anointed for the Attack

"For our struggle is not against flesh and blood, but against the rulers, against the powers, against the world forces of this darkness, against the spiritual forces of wickedness in the heavenly places" Ephesians 6:12.

You are going to face an attack—whether directly from the enemy or through people he influences. But the weapons God gives you have divine power to defeat the devil, demons, and their schemes. They also empower you to gain victory over your own spiritual, mental, and physical struggles. James 4:7 brings comfort: "Be subject therefore unto God; but resist the devil, and he will flee from you. Draw nigh to God, and he will draw nigh to you." Yet there are times when the devil won't leave you alone, and you'll need to stand and fight. A bully doesn't back down until you confront him.

In the same way, Satan, like a roaring lion, only retreats when faced with the Power of Christ. Once he realizes you are aware of his tactics and know how to use the weapons God has given you, he flees. The devil and his demonic minions are no match for the Father, Son, the Holy Spirit, and the heavenly host that God sends to fight on your behalf.

7 DIVINE POWERS TO WAGE WAR

"God doesn't want to save you from the battle; He wants to show you how to win." ~Scott Hogle

The most painful attacks come from those you trust. It's the attacks from within that weaken us the most. They cause us to question ourselves, our instincts, and God. I've gone through seasons where friends turned out to be foes. On one occasion, a company and group of people I trusted turned on me; they became the Accuser of the Brethren. I was under immense pressure—facing constant stress, and there were even career casualties and medical consequences during this season of battle. So, what is the enemy's goal when he attacks directly or through others? To discredit you, weaken you so you stumble or sin, and push you to give up on your assignment. If the enemy can get you to forfeit your assignment, he has won. But remember, the weapons we fight with are not the weapons of the world. On the contrary, they have <u>Divine Power</u> to demolish strongholds (2 Corinthians 10:4). When you go to war, use the divine powers already at your disposal. Don't show up to a gunfight with a knife when you're in the heat of battle. These divine powers include:

1. **Power in Secret Strategy & Scriptures:** When attacked, I sought the Lord for insight and direction. God pointed me to the story of Daniel in the Lion's Den; the scenario involved a set-up, false accusations, and public conviction according to law, and while being surrounded by lions, he had to hold on to his faith. This scripture painted a vivid picture of my own situation.

When I asked God what I should do, His response was clear: "Stay out of it; let Me handle it." It was tough to follow this instruction, but I chose to trust Him and obey. When undergoing an attack, going to God for a story or verse from Scripture and a divine instruction will provide you with a strategy that will help you stay the course and cross the finish line in victory. God will always provide a secret strategy, scripture, and a period of silence while you navigate through your battle. God doesn't remove the fight; He teaches you how to win.

2. **Power in NUMBERS:** Never fight alone. *"One can put a thousand to flight, two can put ten thousand"* (Deuteronomy 32:30). Gathering faith-filled people to intercede for you will strengthen you while unleashing angels in heaven to do battle on your behalf.

3. **Power in THE NAME OF JESUS:** *"At the name of Jesus, every knee bows and tongue confesses that Jesus is Lord"* (Philippians 2:10). Satan can't read your mind, <u>but he can hear your command</u>. If you're praying and need to take authority and bind the enemy, shift from prayer to giving a direct command. For example, command, "Satan, in the name of Jesus, I command you to…" *"Behold, I have given you authority to walk on snakes and scorpions, and authority over all the power of the enemy, and nothing will injure you"* (Luke 10:19). Once Satan realizes you understand and know how to use your authority, he flees in terror.

4. **Power in AGREEMENT:** Jesus said it this way, *"For where two or three have gathered together in My name, I am there in their midst"* (Matthew 18:20). *"A cord of*

three strands is not easily broken" (Ecclesiastes 4:12). When praying or waging war, I find like-minded believers who I can ask to come into agreement with me and to stand with me. Your spouse is the first person you must seek agreement with, as a house that is not in agreement or divided is weakened. We are told to do all we can do, then to STAND. It's important to find believers who will STAND with you in the spirit.

5. **Power in WORSHIP:** There is power in the presence of God during personal and corporal worship. It is through song in the spirit that we are filled with the Spirit, experience the fruits of the Spirit, and have the strength to follow the Spirit. If you are feeling weak, get yourself into worship with others and let the Holy Spirit strengthen you. Doing a daily prayer walk or finding a theme song provides strength during a season of attack.

6. **Power in Quoting The Word of God Out Loud:** When Jesus was tempted in the desert by Satan, he defeated him three times with the same powerful strategy. He countered every twisted truth with the Truth of God's Word. The Word of God is the Sword of the Spirit, and when you wield it, you destroy false arguments that invade your mind. When I start to feel off, I examine the thoughts behind those feelings. By taking <u>every thought captive</u> to the obedience of Christ, as the Bible instructs, I can identify the mental arguments flooding my mind. Then, I sift through them to discern what is from God and what is not. Using God's Word, I can demolish any stronghold—any thought or mindset— that contradicts His Word.

7. **Power in the ARMOR:** When I armor up, I speak out loud as I visualize each piece of the Armor of God as I "put them on." This is how I clothe myself spiritually in this supernatural suit. I say it like this: "Lord, I put on the helmet of salvation to guard my thoughts, the breastplate of righteousness to guard my heart, I walk with the Gospel under my feet to guide my steps, and the belt of truth around my waist so I will not be deceived. I wage war using the Sword of the Spirit, which is the Word of God, and pick up the shield of Faith to extinguish any fiery darts the evil one might fire my way." (Ref. Ephesians 6:14-17)

BATTLES ARE BRIDGES TO A NEW FUTURE

"Indeed, all who want to live in a godly way in Christ Jesus will be persecuted." 2nd Timothy 3:12.

You are anointed for the attack because the Anointer is with you. It's only a matter of time before you find yourself waging war against the powers of darkness. Are you getting stronger or weaker during your seasons of struggle and testing? Kelly Clarkson, the famous pop singer, has a song that says, "What doesn't kill ya makes ya stronger." I have found that to be a half-truth. You have to CHOOSE to garner strength for the storm, and the only way to do that is to keep your eyes on the Savior. Even the Apostle Peter began to sink in the storm when he took his eyes off Jesus. David not only kept his eyes on God, but he also kept INQUIRING of the Lord and asking questions for every battle he faced. Like David, you can experience victory if you let God guide you through your battles.

Let trauma be your tutor. That difficult season brought significant losses, but it also came with invaluable lessons that still guide me today. I've realized that the wisdom gained then is crucial for navigating my future challenges. No matter what I face, I can move from strength to strength by focusing on the Father, not my fear. David, too, was strengthened by the struggles he faced, and God turned his battles into bridges that forged a path toward his Divine Destiny. In what ways is God using your battles to forge a bridge to your next season? Remember, every time you are triumphant in the battles you face, God is glorified, the angels applaud, and you qualify to level up in the natural and the spiritual.

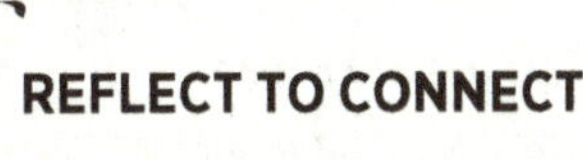

REFLECT TO CONNECT

1. What battles are you facing?
2. What weapons of warfare are you familiar with?
3. Who can you stand in agreement with when praying?

Daughters of the Covenant

"Then the daughters of Zelophehad, the son of Hepher, the son of Gilead, the son of Machir, the son of Manasseh, of the families of Manasseh, the son of Joseph, came near; and these are the names of his daughters: Mahlah, Noah and Hoglah and Milcah and Tirzah. They stood before Moses and before Eleazar, the priest, and before the leaders and all the congregation, at the doorway of the tent of meeting, saying, 'Our father died in the wilderness, yet he was not among the company of those who gathered themselves together against the LORD in the company of Korah; but he died in his own sin, and he had no sons. Why should the name of our father be withdrawn from among his family because he had no son? Give us a possession among our father's brothers.' So Moses brought their case before the LORD" Numbers 27:1-5.

In ancient times, women didn't have the same rights as men. Without legal ownership of property, they faced serious trouble if their husbands passed away—and many did. Yet, this story reveals God's heart for equality and the importance of standing up for yourself. It's a powerful reminder to make your case boldly before both man and God. Five generations after Joseph had died, so Zelophehad died. With no male heir to claim the land in the Promised Land, the daughters of Zelophehad faced exclusion when the territory was divided. But these women weren't just daughters of their earthly father—they were daughters of the Most High, daughters of the covenant. This gave them standing before God, who listened and responded to their prayers. As daughters of the promise, they knew they had to step up and speak out, or they risked being left out.

THE LIMITS YOU OVERCOME DETERMINE WHO YOU BECOME

"God can't send a man to do a woman's job,
you and you alone must step into your Divine Destiny."
~Scott Hogle

Have you been over-looked? The daughters of Zelophehad approached Moses to make their case for the property they were promised. Imagine the intimidation factor, having to stand up before Moses and the elders of Israel to state their case. These women of God acted with boldness. You may not be comfortable stepping up, raising your hand, or defending yourself, but there will be times when you need to speak up for yourself. There will be times when you will need to overcome your upbringing, culture, timidness or shyness, and be bold. There is a time to be quiet and a time to speak up and be heard. In ancient times, women were taught to "know thy place," but these daughters of Zelophehad knew their God. They knew who they were, what they had coming to them, and that God would be their judge and defender. Acting with bravery, the Daughters of Zelophehad stepped forward, and Moses took their case to God. And God said, *"Then the LORD spoke to Moses, saying, 'The daughters of Zelophehad are right in their statements. You shall surely give*

*them a hereditary possession among their father's brothers,
and you shall transfer the inheritance of their father to them'"*
(Numbers 27:6-7). God changed property rights laws because
these courageous women spoke up. *They helped not only
themselves but future generations of women because they
acted boldly. They had to go against the grain and speak
up against the culture and laws of that day.* The steps you
take, the stands you make, and the statements you proclaim
may one day pave the way for generations too. It may start
with a courageous step God prompts you to take. Is there a
circumstance in which you need to be bold? God can't send
a man to do a woman's job, there are some steps you must
take to walk in your Divine Destiny.

GOD FAVORS OVERCOMERS

*"The one who overcomes, I will confess his name before My
Father and before His angels."* (Ref. Revelation 3:5)

My mother's brother, Tim, married wisely. While they dated,
Cecilia would ask Tim about God, and Tim would answer.
They had many conversations where Tim shared stories from
the Bible and explained the ways of the Lord. But after they
married, as Cecilia drew closer to God, Tim began to drift
away. God would use a shy woman of great faith to pray
Tim back into the fold. Day and night, Cecilia interceded for
Tim, boldly entering the Throne Room of Grace to plead her
case. Her prayers didn't go unanswered—one day, as Tim
watched a Christian televangelist, he experienced a dramatic
healing that brought him back to Christ. God's promise to
Tim's parents would be fulfilled, *"Train up a child in the way*

he should go, and when he is old, he will not depart from it"
(Proverbs 22:6).

Do you know what your standing is before God? Together, they would do great work for God by traveling the world as broadcast evangelists. Like the daughters of Zelophehad, Cecilia is bold and courageous, but she wasn't always that way. Raised in an Asian culture where women were subservient to men and not permitted to speak unless spoken to, she would have to bravely adapt to American culture to fulfill God's potential for her life. God made her an intercessor and prayer warrior, spending hours each day in quiet prayer. But when she is serving in the healing rooms, a boldness comes out of her when she steps forward, speaks up, and proclaims the power and promises of God over those in need of healing. She is so quiet that you may not know she is in the room at times, but just ask her a question about the goodness of God and watch her rise up. She is a woman of faith who knows her STANDING BEFORE GOD. When Cecilia is fulfilling her role as an intercessor prayer warrior, the Spirit of God transforms her. Energized by prayer, she changes from being shy and quiet to boldly proclaiming God's power and promises to those seeking healing. The women of Zelophehad stood up to state their case before God. Cecilia speaks up to proclaim God's power and healing over people. What has God called you to step forward into?

REFLECT TO CONNECT

1. What courageous conversations is God prompting you to have?
2. When have you been over-looked and had to speak up for yourself or another?
3. In what ways do you need to overcome your cultural upbringing or circumstance to become who God has called you to be?

The Places of Destiny

*"This is the Word that came to Jeremiah from the Lord,
'Go to the potter's house, and THERE I will reveal
My message to you'"* Jeremiah 18:1-2.

There are specific places where God calls us to go. Some places are meant for seeing, others for hearing, gaining perspective, or receiving. Certain places make it easier for God to reach us. While God can deliver a message to you anywhere, He carefully considers your mindset, frame of reference, and worldview to ensure you receive His Word in the most impactful way possible.

The Potter's House was a Place of Perspective, a reference point that God chose specifically to reveal to Jeremiah. Do you have a place where you feel especially close and connected to God? For me, that connection is strongest during my devotional quiet time. There have been seasons in my life—between jobs or traveling—when I unexpectedly stumbled upon a place where I deeply felt the presence of God. God led Israel with a cloud by day and a fire by night so they would know when to start or stop and when to remain in a place. Places are important to God. He made places before He made people. What place is God calling you to stay, visit, or move to? You will hear Him best in the place of His calling. As God directed Jeremiah to go to a place to receive a new perspective, He may want to move you to shift your perspective. God told

Elijah to go to a brook named Cherith for provision, then sent him to a widow at Zarephath to provide for him. God may change your place from time to time. There is a place of purpose where you will fulfill His plans for your life.

Where is the PLACE that makes God's presence feel the strongest in your life? For a season, your place may be a daily prayer walk, on the top of a mountain, or a cliff overlooking the ocean. Where is your potter's house? Jacob met God in a dream while traveling, and Jacob named that place Bethel, which means "house of God." Bethel became a place where Jacob would seek and experience God when he passed through that region. Bethel became a place where Jacob intersected with God. One of the places I like to meet with God is on extended road trips. In GOD WINKS & WINDSHIELD WORSHIP, I mention that I seek God during my daily commute and long road trips. God can speak to you anywhere, yet there are some places where your spirit is more sensitized to His Spirit. Here are a few examples of places God may speak to you about.

7 PLACES OF ASSIGNMENT

"God sets the times and places of your habitation."
Ref. Acts 17:26

1. **PLACES OF ASSIGNMENT: Remain in the place you feel God's presence.** Have you ever felt like the pastor on the stage was speaking directly to you? There is a reason you feel drawn to some places and not others. Just as the Israelites followed the cloud by day and the fire by night, sensing God's presence is a sign of where He wants you to stay. When God's Spirit repeatedly resonates with you in one place over another, that's a strong indication of where Jesus wants you to abide in that season. My oldest son, Bailey, once came home after attending a men's group at a different church than our home church. He was deeply moved by the connection he felt with the pastor and the men there. As he shared his experience encountering God in that place, I knew he had found his calling for that season of his life. Where you feel God's presence the strongest is a clue to where you belong.

2. **THE PLACE OF HONOR + FAVOR: Go where you are celebrated, not tolerated.** Early in my career, I found good mentors and success, and God was blessing the work of my hands. Then everything changed. The company I worked for was sold and my mentors moved on, as did the favor I experienced. The new bosses didn't value my input like the old ones did. I could feel an emotional shift in the atmosphere. What changed? Honor and favor dried up in that PLACE; it was God's

signal to me that it was time to move on, so I did. There is a place of honor and favor where you will experience God's hand on you and fruitfulness in your life. On the flip side, you can also find yourself in a place of famine, and God will use that famine to move you as He did Elijah when He told him to leave the brook. When you are in the place you belong, you know it, and when you are not, you know it. When Jesus sent the 70 out, He instructed them to remain in the places where they found favor and acceptance and to depart the places where they didn't. He told them to shake the dust off their feet and depart. Jesus followed His own advice when He could not perform miracles in His hometown of Nazareth, so He left and went to Capernaum, where His ministry took off. When favor and honor are lacking where you are, that may be a clue that God is moving you.

3. **THE PLACE OF OBEDIENCE: If you have not felt God lately, go back to the place you last felt Him.** Has God ever said "NO" to you as you sought His guidance? If He is saying "NO," it is because He sees something in your future that could steer you away from your Divine Destiny. If you push beyond His Will, you might find yourself stepping out from under His covering. If you no longer feel God's hand guiding your life, return to the place and last "decision" you made when you sensed His presence. He will be there, waiting for you in the Place of Obedience.

4. **THE PLACE OF CONTACT AND INSTRUCTION: The Word of God is your Manna from heaven,**

your daily portion, your contact point with God.
While in the desert, Israel relied on God for 40 years
to feed them with Manna from heaven. Each day, God
gave them exactly what they needed; their "daily bread"
to sustain them. In the same way, God provides daily
bread to those who show up at His table. Jesus said,
"Man shall not live by bread alone, but by every Word
that proceeds from the mouth of God." Each day, God
has a portion set aside just for you, perfectly tailored
for what you will face that day. This daily portion is
His gift to you—your Manna from heaven, a spiritual
provision for the journey ahead. Every morning, as I
read Scripture, I search for that one verse that truly
resonates with my spirit. I am listening for a whisper
from the Word or a sudden unction to do something
or call someone. When something begins to resonate,
I know I have found my contact point with God for
that day, my daily bread. When a thought or person
comes to mind while you're in God's presence, that is
your contact point for the day—your daily bread. In
IMAGINATE WITH GOD, you read about how God
used a picture and Scripture at a conference to direct
my brother where to find provision. His place of Provision on two occasions was at a conference, listening to
spirit-inspired speakers.

"But ye have an unction from the Holy One,
and ye know all things." 1 John 2:20 (KJV)

5. **PLACE OF ANOINTING: There is a fresh anointing
waiting for you in your place of assignment.** In the

mid-1990s, Pastor Wayne Cordeiro successfully led New Hope Church in Hilo, Hawaii. God asked him to leave that place and go to Oahu to start over. Pastor Wayne wrestled with that decision as God had blessed him and his church in Hilo. So why would God ask Wayne to go somewhere else and start over? Because his Place of Assignment had changed. When you are where you belong, doing what God wants you to do, you are in the PLACE OF ANOINTING. There is a place of supernatural fruitfulness that enters your life when you enter the PLACE OF ANOINTING. Since Pastor Wayne followed God's instructions to go to Honolulu, over 150 New Hope churches have been planted worldwide, and almost 100,000 souls have come to Jesus. One man's step of obedience would land him in a Place of Anointing where God's fruitfulness and favor continue to multiply into eternity. Where is the place of anointing you feel God's hand at work in your life?

> *"In the place of anointing, there is a multiplication of fruitfulness that spills over into multiple areas of your life."* ~Scott Hogle

6. **PLACE OF HEALING & REMEMBERANCE: There are PLACES where you will receive an impartation that links to your Divine Destiny.** In 2018, while I was battling cancer, I saw a TV announcement promoting a Healing is Here conference at Andrew Wommack's Ministry in Woodland Park, Colorado. I limped into the kitchen and told my wife I felt we needed to go. Two

weeks later, we were on a plane. I went seeking healing, not just to attend a conference. I received both a healing and a teaching, and I spent the next six months living out what I had learned. For me, the Place of Healing and impartation began at a healing conference. God used that place to set me on the path to healing. Because it was where I encountered God in a new and powerful way, my wife Kate and I still visit it from time to time to remember and thank God for what He did. Is there a place that was a turning point for you, where you met God in a special way?

7. **PLACE OF VULNERABILITY: People respect you for your strength, but they connect with you and God when you share your struggles.** Years ago, I had a breakfast meeting with my brother Steve, and it became a Place of Vulnerability. While we were eating, Steve became verbally and visibly upset with me. When I asked what was wrong, he said, "You never open up and share with me." Steve was struggling to connect with me and was frustrated that I didn't share the things I was struggling with. It wasn't that I didn't want to share; I just handled my difficulties and struggles differently. I don't typically openly share or express my emotions—I only talk to my wife and God about them. *But the Lord shared with me that when I withhold my fears, struggles, and weaknesses, it takes away God's ability*

to use my testimonies to help others. I learned that it is through personal struggles that people connect and get closer to God. People respect you for your strength, but they connect with you and God when you share your struggles. The willingness to be vulnerable helps people walk through their pain and experience the manifold grace of God. I will never forget what Steve said to me that day. It changed my life, and I am intentional (not comfortable) about sharing my failures, struggles, and weaknesses with others so they have a runway to connect with God. I now resonate with the Apostle Paul when he said, *"Most gladly therefore will I rather glory in my weaknesses, that the power of Christ may rest upon me."* Where is the best place to do this? In the Place of Vulnerability.

REFLECT TO CONNECT

1. Where is the Place God is leading you to go?
2. What type of Place—spiritual or physical—do you feel most connected to?
3. Where were you when you had your most profound, life-changing encounter with God?

Desperately Seeking God

"Then Elkanah, her husband, said to her, 'Hannah, why do you weep and why do you not eat and why is your heart sad? Am I not better to you than ten sons?' Then Hannah rose after eating and drinking in Shiloh. Now Eli the priest was sitting on the seat by the doorpost of the temple of the LORD. She, greatly distressed, prayed to the LORD and wept bitterly. She made a vow and said, 'Oh LORD of hosts, if You will indeed look on the affliction of Your maidservant and remember me, and not forget Your maidservant, but will give Your maidservant a son, then I will give him to the LORD all the days of his life, and a razor shall never come on his head'" 1 Samuel 1:8-11.

God may ordain a season of seeking for you. Hannah sought a son, but God had something much greater in store for her. When you pray, remember that you're speaking to a kind and loving Father *"who is able to do far more abundantly beyond all that we ask or think, according to the power that works within us"* (Ephesians 3:20). What drove Hannah to desperately seek God? She was barren year after year, and in ancient Israel, a woman who couldn't bear children often felt deep shame. This prolonged pain pushed Hannah into a season of fervent seeking. God promises that we will find Him when we seek Him with all our heart, and Hannah was about to experience this truth. She devised a plan to go to a new place to seek God, setting aside time and making a deliberate effort to find Him. Have you ever dedicated a specific time or place to seek God? In the PLACES OF DESTINY devotion, you read about how certain places hold special significance to God. For Hannah, it wasn't just the place but the desperation of her heart that broke through and brought her into God's presence.

"Lord, how do you want to use my situation?" Hannah asked God for a child, but God had even bigger plans for her. He not only granted her request but also blessed her with a son, Samuel, who would grow up to become one of Israel's greatest prophets. What are you seeking in this season? While searching for an answer, God might prepare you to receive far more than you imagine. The key to getting the most out of your season of seeking is to ask, "Lord, how do You want to use my situation?"

In the radio business, sometimes you have to adjust your receiver to pick up a signal. An engineer needs to SHIFT the direction of the antenna to pick up what is being transmitted. In what ways is God leading you to make a SHIFT? Do you need to adjust your antenna? Who and what are you tuning into?

THE AMAZING RACE

Where is your next set of instructions? "The Amazing Race" is a TV show where teams of two compete against each other, traveling from city to city and country to country. Along the way, they reach CHECK POINTS, where they pick up instructions for the next leg of their journey. The race is challenging, and the conditions unbearable at times. Participants strive not only to succeed, but at times, just survive. Each team follows the instructions they've been given until they reach the next CHECK POINT, where they receive the next set of instructions. The team that reaches the final destination first wins the race. So, what is the last instruction from God that you're currently following?

TRAVELING TO MEET WITH GOD

"Getting you out of your comfort zone and into a new environment is often God's way to get you out of the way of what He's trying to do in and through you."

How might God be leading you to find your next CHECK POINT? God promised in Psalm 34:17-18, *"The righteous cry out, and the LORD hears and rescues them from all their troubles. The LORD is near to the brokenhearted and saves those who are crushed in spirit."* Have you ever wept bitterly to God in anguish like Hannah? Have you ever gone out of your way to seek God out of desperation? My wife Kate is a successful entrepreneur who owns and operates an advertising agency, serves in Women's Ministry, and juggles the roles of mom and wife. But a few years ago, she was struggling. She felt stretched thin, overwhelmed, and desperate for change. During this challenging season, she was invited to travel to Atlanta, Georgia, for a women's conference. God wasn't just calling her to a place of self-care; He was leading her to a place of renewal and restoration. She returned a changed woman with a fresh anointing for her life.

As a husband, the best advice I can give men is to send their wives to conferences and girlfriend trips and support any opportunity their wives have to be refreshed. For Kate, she came back changed and on fire to serve Christ in a new way. When women get together in the Spirit, there is a strengthening and transfer that happens to unlock the next leg of their Divine Destiny. Kate found a new CHECK POINT and a new touch point with God. Like Hannah, she found her "Eli and Shiloh" with a Christian coach named Lori Salierno-Maldonado at a Wild Women of God Conference in Atlanta. God can reach you exactly where you are, and you don't need to travel to find God. That said, getting out of your comfort zone and into a new environment is a powerful way to get *out of the way* of what God wants to do. Removing the interference and strongholds that block God's best is more easily done in a new setting.

Everyone seeks something; what are you on the hunt for? Being obedient to the Lord's leading can UNLOCK God's best for you. What Kate did not know at the time was that one step of faith, going <u>out of her way</u> to seek God, would unlock currents of favor and blessing for her. This one <u>act of obedience</u> took her from a season of seeking to a season of strength. Whenever God wants to do something in your life, <u>He will bring you to a place and a person</u>. God used Kate's single decision to seek Him to transform her completely—as a businesswoman, an owner, a wife, and a mother. Paul sought Jesus in the desert of Arabia. Moses sought God at Sinai and Jacob at a place named Bethel, where God met with him. Where does God want to meet with you? What new relationships does He want to birth in your life? Get ready to SHIFT.

REFLECT TO CONNECT

1. In what way is God trying to SHIFT you so you can receive from Him?
2. How might your receiver need to be retuned or recalibrated so you can receive from God?
3. Where is your next CHECK POINT? Is there a place where you can pick up your next set of instructions?

The Emotional Will of God

"Delight yourself in the LORD; And He will give you the desires of your heart"

Psalm 37:4.

God feels deeply and passionately. God can be wounded by you. In fact, we are instructed, *"Do not grieve the Holy Spirit of God, by whom you were sealed for the day of redemption"* (Ephesians 4:30). Another very powerful emotion God exhibits is jealousy. God describes Himself as a "jealous God." He won't share your worship with false gods. God is as much of an emotional creature as you and I. One way He communicates with you is emotionally, in the depths of your heart, where He lives. He will allow you to feel what He feels so you can see and do what He desires through you. God gives you His desire, so you will know what His heart is in a situation or toward a certain someone. This is critical to understanding and interpreting how the heart of God moves upon you.

"For this is the covenant that I will make with the house of Israel after those days, saith the Lord; I will put my laws into their mind, and write them in their hearts: and I will be to them a God, and they shall be to me a people: And they shall not teach every man his neighbor, and every man his brother, saying, Know the Lord: for all shall know me, from the least to the greatest." Hebrews 8:10-11

God desires intimacy with you! From the beginning, God planned to live inside of you and give you His heart so you could live together forever in deep intimacy and communion. What could be more intimate than when God's heart becomes your heart, and you become one? It is then that His heart on a matter is unmistakable. God giving you the desire of your heart doesn't mean He will give you that new BMW you have your eye on. It means that His desires will imprint over your heart, so you desire what He desires; His heart becomes your heart. My wife and I like many of the same things. I know her mind on food, travel, work, ministry, and so much more. Because we are one in marriage, the intimacy and daily experience of living together have merged our hearts. She has a saying, "The older we get, the more I become like you." I've noticed that the older I get, the more I become like her. Over time, our hearts are imprinted on each other. Some people say that older couples start to resemble each other after spending a lifetime together. It's just another way of seeing how, over time, two people truly become one. Following are some of the most common ways God reveals His Will through your emotions.

THE HOLY HEART FLIP

"Moreover, I will give you a new heart and put a new spirit within you; and I will remove the heart of stone from your flesh and give you a heart of flesh." Ezekial 36:26

When God gives you the desires of your heart, His heart becomes your heart, so you know His mind toward a situation or someone. Have you ever <u>been set in your thinking</u>

on a subject or someone, but then all of a sudden, you had a change of heart? I call this the HOLY HEART FLIP. My friends Dee and Bryan met many years ago at church. From the get-go, Bryan loved Dee and wanted to marry her, but Dee didn't feel the same way. Dee tells the story that when she and Bryan first met, she had no thoughts about marriage. But then God changed her heart. After a few months of dating, she felt that Bryan was getting serious, but she didn't feel the same way. She was a new believer, but even then, she knew to seek God and ask what He desired for her. She asked directly and boldly, "If this is who You desire me to be with, You will need to change my heart." And God did.

What happened? Dee experienced a HOLY HEART FLIP and God's heart toward Bryan became her heart. When God's heart becomes your heart, you feel what God feels. It's not forced; it's an unmistakable holy emotion welling up within you. You feel one way about a situation or someone, but now you feel the opposite. What you didn't prefer, you now prefer; what you once said you'd never do, you are now doing; what you hated, you now like; what you said you didn't want to do, you now have a desire to do. What happened? Your heart flipped. If you are seeking God and all of a sudden, you experience a HEART FLIP, that is evidence of God directing your steps. Be aware, however, of getting a desire that contradicts God's Word or nature; anything that contradicts the Bible or God's character is not from God.

Another way you can tell who or what influences you is that God invites while the enemy pushes. Have you ever experienced a HOLY HEART FLIP? It's when your feelings about something completely change, often in surprising ways.

Maybe there was a place you never wanted to move to, but now you feel drawn to it—that's a Holy Heart Flip. Or perhaps you once resisted the idea of doing something, and now you find yourself wanting it—that's another Holy Heart Flip. It's when what you were once certain about suddenly reverses. This is more than just a change of mind; it's God's heart becoming your heart as He reveals His will to you.

HOLY EMOTIONS

"As you feel touched with holy compassion, it is God's way of prompting you to be His touch toward someone." ~Scott Hogle

Have you ever experienced a strong emotional DRAW to someone, someplace, or something? The Apostle Paul once had a dream of a man in Macedonia waving to him and asking him to come and help. Paul felt DRAWN to help the man and concluded the Holy Spirit was pointing him in a new direction. It wasn't just the dream but the emotional DRAW Paul felt that compelled him to change direction and head to Macedonia. God will use holy emotions so you feel drawn to help the people He wants to help through you. Paul never met the man from Macedonia, but he did meet a woman named Lydia. As Paul preached by the water, God opened Lydia's heart; she was DRAWN to his message and DRAWN to serve and provide for Paul and his friends. Lydia experienced God's heart toward Paul and his traveling companions. In Matthew 14:14, *"Jesus went out, and He saw a great multitude; and He was MOVED with compassion for them, and healed their sick."* This holy compassion was God's holy emotion directing Jesus.

It is through holy emotions that God's heart for someone or something will become your heart. As you feel touched with holy compassion, listen; this is God's way of prompting you to be His touch toward someone. When you feel DRAWN to act on God's behalf, God is inviting you to be the hands, feet, voice, or touch of Jesus. Holy emotions are one of the ways that God guides. Who or what are you feeling a holy compassion toward? Where or to whom is God drawing you?

HOLY DREAMS

"And it shall come to pass afterward, that I will pour out My Spirit upon all flesh; and your sons and your daughters shall prophesy, your old men shall dream dreams, your young men shall see visions." Joel 2:28

It's time to dream with God. You read earlier how Paul Malijewsky was given many God-given dreams throughout his life. On one occasion, he contemplated moving to Florida, but then God gave him a dream and showed him that he would be moving to Hemet, California, and he did. In each instance, he picked up his family and moved to the location God showed him in the dream. This sort of dream is a directional dream. Steve Sombrero had a God-given dream where he was given a math equation. That dream remained pregnant in his spirit and would be birthed into a book one day. Joseph, like Steve, was given a dream as a youth that would not materialize until 13 years later when he became the Governor of Egypt. If you've ever woken from a dream with a burden on your heart to call or write someone, these are what I call "holy dreams." God may use dreams to prompt you or warn you. For years, I had a recurring dream of moving my family to another state and taking a new job. The dream always ended the same way, with me regretting my decision. I knew this was a warning from God not to be enticed with promotion, pay, or anything that would move me out of His will. Has God given you a dream that is recurring, prompting, or feels like a warning? Has God ever given you a dream to get your attention? God once used a dream to do a miracle in my life.

On one occasion, I received a healing miracle while in a waking dream state. I was in the middle of a brutal bout with cancer and had lost my ability to walk. The cancer had eaten through the bone in my lower right leg, and the X-ray showed that the bone was gone. I had been on a knee scooter for a long time. Each morning, I would awake surprised that God had not healed me. There came a moment, months into my journey, when I told God, "I've read all the books on healing and meditated on all the Scriptures. You're going to have to do the rest." I was frustrated and waiting on God, but I also focused on staying in faith. Early one morning, I had a waking dream where I saw myself throwing my knee scooter aside and starting to run. Instantly, I woke from the dream, and I knew I would be able to walk that day. I went into the kitchen and my wife looked at me in shock and asked, "What are you doing!?" I said, "I'm walking!" and I've been walking ever since. A month later, I went back to the doctor for another X-ray, but the bone had not grown back. You might be wondering how I was walking. I was walking on faith. People still ask if I have ever gone back for an X-ray to confirm whether or not the bone grew back, and I always tell them the same thing, "No, what does it matter? I'm walking." I have only had a few holy dreams in my life; however, I have woken many times with the burden of doing something or calling someone. Pay particular attention to your waking moments as God will whisper in your spirit a holy desire at a time when your mind is clear and uncluttered yet by the day's activities.

REFLECT TO CONNECT

1. Is there a dream God keeps bringing to you?
2. In what instance has God's compassion flooded your heart, directing you to help someone?
3. When have you experienced a HOLY HEART FLIP where your heart was changed toward a person or situation?

Stirred by the Energy of the Holy

"Now in the first year of Cyrus, king of Persia, in order to fulfill the Word of the LORD by the mouth of Jeremiah, the LORD <u>stirred up the spirit of Cyrus,</u> so that he sent a proclamation throughout his kingdom This is what Cyrus king of Persia says: 'The LORD, the God of heaven, has given me all the kingdoms of the earth, and He has appointed me to rebuild for Him a house in Jerusalem, which is in Judah. Whoever there is among you of all His people, may his God be with him! Go up to Jerusalem which is in Judah and rebuild the house of the LORD, the God of Israel; He is the God who is in Jerusalem'"
Ezra 1:1-3.

When God wants to MOVE you, He will STIR you. When God moved in the heart of Cyrus, it sparked a chain reaction—Cyrus was driven to action and, in turn, inspired others to join him. This is a holy prompting, an unction from the Holy urging you to step into action. For Cyrus, that stirring ignited a new desire and a clear instruction: rebuild the temple in Jerusalem. He was given not just a mission but a vision, rallying the people around him to participate in this God-given project.

In the same way, when God stirs your heart, He provides you with direction, instruction, and the drive to get you moving toward your Divine Destiny. You'll feel an unmistakable, holy energy, much like Samson did when supernatural strength filled him to conquer the Philistines. That stirring within you is a powerful signal—it's time to move, time to act, time to step into what God has planned for you.

God's stirring may be uncomfortable until you respond. God may stir you with a dream or a restless night's sleep. God stirred Pharoah and Nebuchadnezzar with troubling dreams that only Joseph and Daniel could interpret. God gave Joseph the ability to interpret their dreams, and it elevated his position within the secular kingdom in order to become an instrument God could use. He stirred King Xerxes during a sleepless night that prompted the king to read The Chronicles, where he discovered a man named Mordecai, who had once saved his life. This stirring in King Xerxes leads him to put Mordecai in the second most powerful position in Persia. God stirs us to position, reposition, get our attention, and get us moving. God knows how to stir people and He knows how to stir you.

A GENTLE STIRRING IS GOD'S WAY
TO SEE IF YOU WILL ENGAGE

"When you feel God's stirring, He is moving you into position." ~Scott Hogle

How is the STIRRING of the Spirit manifesting in your life? I like to spend the first seven minutes of my devotional time in silence with a blank piece of paper. Sanctifying the first few minutes of each day to the Lord in solitude is my way of putting God first. My spirit is quiet upon waking, my bandwidth reserve is full, and the focused solitude helps me to sensitize my spirit to His stirring. What am I listening for? A holy stirring. Why is this important? Because God can accomplish in a day what it takes you a decade. He can inspire you with an idea that will unlock increases in influence, income, favor, relationship access, healing, and more. While the Holy Spirit desires to stir you, He desires that you will also stir Him. He is stirred with worship, inward reciting in song or Psalms, and when reading and meditating on the Word of God. These moments ignite the Holy Spirit within you. Once He is stirred, He will guide you—prompting your thoughts, actions, and words. His stirring will open your eyes, ears, and heart in ways you may never have experienced before. To align yourself with His direction, here are a few questions to bring into your quiet time, helping you and the Holy Spirit move together.

7 MINUTES OF SILENCE

"To me they listened and waited,
And they kept silent for my advice." Job 29:21

1. **What am I excited about in this season of life?** Where there is a holy desire and energy, God is stirring you into action. When God's desire becomes your desire, you will be moved by what moves Him. God's stirring is directional, to move you through the next door. Where are you being led?

2. **What is my pain point?** Pain is a clue to a conversation that God wants to have with you. C.S. Lewis said, "God whispers to us in our pleasure but shouts at us in our pain." Pain is a way for God to get your attention

when you have not been listening. Where is the pain stirring in your life?

3. **What questions can I ask God?** Writing your questions out on paper will unlock a new dialogue between you and God. A question, when asked and meditated on, will create a dialogue within you. I ask God questions about my day, my struggles, and my opportunities. Some He answers immediately, and some unfold over time, as God knows the deadlines in our lives. Once stirred in this way, you will never be the same. What questions do you have for God today?

4. **God, what are You heavy-hearted about?** The holy burden you feel is an invitation from God to ease His pain toward a person, place, or circumstance. The moment you move toward the burden, the burden starts to lift. This is His way of confirming that you are moving in the right direction.

5. **What idea is coming to mind for the problem I am facing?** An inspired idea is God's way of giving you an instruction that will unlock a solution for you. As you think about your problem in the presence of God, pay particular attention to what stirs within you. Be careful not to dismiss an idea that may seem ridiculous. Sometimes, God gives one thought to get you to think in a direction so He can plant the right thought in the garden of your mind.

6. **Where is the energy, adrenaline, or urgency in my life TODAY?** When God wants to prompt you, He may use an event in your life to poke you in order to get you moving. When an angel came to break the Apostle

Peter out of jail, the Scripture says that the angel "struck Peter" in his side to wake him up. If you're anything like me, sometimes it takes a little nudge to push you out of your comfort zone and move you in the direction God is calling you. Where are you feeling that nudge right now?

7. **What questions are coming to my mind?** Sometimes, to get your attention, God will pose a question. To Hagar, God asked, "Where have you come from and where are you going?" This question speaks to purpose, direction, and a frame of reference. To Solomon, He asked, "What can I do for you?" God wants you to verbalize your needs, have you? God asked Adam, "Who told you that you were naked?" God may ask you who you've been listening to lately. Who you listen to affects how you feel. What question is bubbling up in your spirit? If you do not know, ask God for His question and wait to see what is asked.

"Listen to me in silence." Isaiah 41:1

REFLECT TO CONNECT

1. Where is the Holy Energy, the stirring, in your life right now?

2. Is there something that is time-sensitive that God is stirring you about?

3. Is there a daily time of Bible reading and reflection that you can set aside to look and listen for the stirring?

The Faithful Follower

*"For I am confident of this very thing, that He who began
a good work among you will complete it by the day of
Christ Jesus"* Philippians 1:6.

Let the Holy Spirit be your tutor! David Barton, founder of Wall Builders, tells of how school children were taught in America early in its infancy. There were no textbooks, so the Bible was the only textbook used. He explained that if someone was interested in going into banking, they would read the Bible throughout the year and pay special attention to Scriptures that talked about banking, finance, or return on investment. If someone wanted to learn about the building or agriculture industry, as they read the Bible that year, they would pay close attention to Scriptures that touched on farming or construction. The Bible is full of parables, stories, principles, and examples on nearly every subject imaginable. In ancient times, people learned about various professions by studying these divine teachings. You can do the same today by tapping into the unique wiring God has programmed into your mind. When Scripture says you are "fearfully and wonderfully made," the Reticular Activating System (RAS) in your brain is a prime example. This system, gifted to you by God at birth, is your brain's attention center. Whatever you set your attention on, your brain acts like a homing beacon, drawing in the information it seeks. In other words, whatever you focus on becomes magnified—you start to see, hear, and notice everything related to it. The incredible part? You have the power to set and program your RAS. It is by intentionally programming and pointing your focus that you can achieve amazing things with God's help.

Most people do not intentionally use their RAS but accidentally use it. For example, have you ever noticed that when you're in the market to buy a computer, you start to see computer ads everywhere and find yourself noticing people's laptops and computers in your office? Or if you just bought a new red truck, all of a sudden, you notice red trucks everywhere. This isn't magic or coincidence—it's your RAS at work. Now, imagine what you could achieve by intentionally directing your RAS every day.

IT'S TIME TO DEVELOP YOUR SPIRITUAL SKILL SET

"The secret to mastery is to become and remain a student."
~Scott Hogle

Have you discovered the hidden riches in Christ's Word? In my bestselling devotional, *Divine Intelligence,* I describe the Bible as a Spiritual Swiss Army Knife. I've taught many lessons on how to "Persuade like Paul," "Ask Questions like Jesus," "Grow in Favor like Daniel," and "Problem Solve like Joseph." Reading through the Bible while studying these subjects is an example of how I use my RAS to pick up on what God wants me to find. In *Divine Intelligence,* you'll also read about "How to Live Courageously like Joshua," "Develop Faith like Abraham," and "Leverage your Business like Lydia."

Some of my favorite devotionals include "How to Use Your Slingshot Gift Like David" and "How to Develop Emotional Intelligence Like Solomon." Using your RAS while reading the Bible will help you to develop the "mindset of the Master" in no time. You will know the Way of the Lord in many different categories and develop your Spiritual Skill Set.

FEED YOURSELF

"The heart of the wise instructs his mouth and adds persuasiveness to his lips."
Proverbs 16:23

FEED YOURSELF is the mantra founding pastor Wayne Cordeiro preached for years at New Hope Oahu. You and you alone are responsible for your growth. In order to grow up in Christ, you must feed yourself. Just as your body can't survive without nourishment, so your spirit won't grow without the nutrients found in the Word of God. Solomon reminds us that we need to teach ourselves, even instruct ourselves, how to speak if we want to become persuasive when he says in Proverbs 16:23, *"The heart of the wise instructs his mouth and adds persuasiveness to his lips."* This means you are meant to be student-minded and an instructor to yourself. The secret to success is becoming a student. But remember, *who* you learn from is as important as *what* you are learning.

In the first half of my career, I worked in the advertising sales business. As I progressed, there were 4 subjects that I intentionally studied. Based on the calling on my life and how God was using me, I made it a point to become a student of these subjects. I use the acronym S.A.L.T. to explain.

S. Sales: Sales is the study of persuasion, the ability to move people, their thinking, and their actions. Everyone is in the persuasion business; the question is, are you any good at it? Teachers work to hold the student's attention while teaching so they will learn; leaders lead so followers will follow; and artists sing songs so people will buy their albums. Businesses, churches, and governments must have an influx of revenue to stay in business. Would becoming more persuasive be helpful to you in your lane?

A. Attitude: By definition, attitude is a way of thinking, a mindset that leads to feelings and actions. William James, the American psychologist, once said, "The greatest discovery of my generation is that people can control their feelings by controlling their thoughts." When you become a student of how people think, you will be better able to manage the attitudes around you and within you. When you learn to control your own thoughts, you have a mastered life.

L. Leadership: The ability to lead yourself and others will determine your level of effectiveness and success in every aspect of life. The most important person I must lead is myself, followed by my inner circle and then those I have charge over.

T. Theology: As a follower of Christ, I study his Word, the great writers, thinkers, theologians and spiritual thought leaders. This brings me great joy. One of the books that changed my life is called *The Divine Mentor* by Wayne Cordeiro, founder of New Hope International. One of the key premises in the book teaches that the mentors in the Bible were given to us as examples to follow. Their lives, lessons, and stories are given to us to instruct us in the Way of the Lord for our lives. These writers are divine mentors, gifts from God, to help us succeed in our Christian walk. These examples in the scriptures provide divine insight on how to navigate all manners of challenges. *The Divine Mentor* so inspired me that it eventually led me to write my first devotional, *Divine Intelligence*.

WHO ARE YOU BECOMING?

"Follow me as I follow Christ." The Apostle Paul

Everyone follows someone; who are you following? Mentorship is how God trains you up. Throughout Scripture, God uses mentors to develop His children and advance His purposes. Joshua had Moses to mentor him, Joseph had Potipher, and Timothy had Paul. The power of mentorship is found in not just the transfer of knowledge but the transfer of character. There is an imprinting that can happen when close mentoring occurs. Some of the most important lessons I've learned have come from mentors I did not particularly like. I've learned to gain wisdom from both the successes and failures of others, taking note of what they did well and where they fell short.

As you follow Christ, He will guide you on what to embrace and what to leave behind. In the same way that you can intentionally choose what subjects to focus your RAS on, you can choose *who* you will follow and learn from. Whoever you are following and learning from will influence and shape your thoughts. Your thoughts lead to your feelings, and feelings lead to actions, which create your Divine Destiny. The most powerful words ever spoken by Jesus were, "FOLLOW ME." The Apostle Paul would later say, "Follow me as I follow Christ." When you get serious about moving toward your Divine Destiny, you will want to grow in your relationship with Jesus by becoming a student of His Word, His ways, and the mentors He puts on your path. Let me encourage you to seek out experts in the field that aligns with God's Divine Destiny for your life. Learn from them and follow their example.

Throughout each season of my life, I've drawn wisdom from a variety of mentors. One mentor alone isn't enough to make you a subject matter expert in multiple areas. The mentors who guided me in my 20s are not the same ones I turned to in my 30s. The mentors I have today are not the same mentors I had 10 years ago. Like with the change of seasons, you should have seasonal mentors that enter and exit your life. I have never met many of my mentors. Many of their books have changed my life and shaped my thinking. Whatever your lane of assignment, you will level up faster when you find the right Biblical mentors and trusted subject matter experts to follow.

REFLECT TO CONNECT

1. Who has made the most impact on your life and character?
2. Who might God be leading you to learn from in your present season?
3. What subject must you master to fulfill your Divine Destiny?

Just A.S.K.

"So I say to you, ask, and it will be given to you; seek, and you will find; knock, and it will be opened to you. For everyone who asks receives, and the one who seeks finds, and to the one who knocks, it will be opened" Luke 11:9-10.

The three letters in "A.S.K." unlock the power of answered prayer. When the disciples asked Jesus, "Lord, teach us to pray," He shared with them the Lord's Prayer. But then, Jesus simplified it even further: **Ask, Seek, Knock.** It's as if He was giving them an insider's secret to how prayer works.

The Greek word Jesus used for "ask" is Aieto, which means to DEMAND. Imagine Jesus inviting you to step into God's presence and boldly make a demand—would you have the courage to do it? Yet, that's exactly what Hebrews 4:16 encourages: *"Let us therefore come <u>boldly</u> unto the throne of grace, that we may obtain mercy, and find grace to help in time of need"* (KJV).

As a child of God, you have the right to approach Him boldly, just like a family member with full standing. Just as a loving parent encourages their child to stand up, speak out, and be heard, God is urging you to do the same.

ASK – SEEK – KNOCK

"You have not because you ask not." ~ Jesus

Just ask, then do what God tells you. In the Old Testament, people went to prophets to present their cases before God. One such woman, a daughter of God, found herself in desperate need. She courageously approached the prophet Elisha with a bold demand: *"Now a woman of the wives of the sons of the prophets cried out to Elisha, saying, 'Your servant my husband is dead, and you know that your servant feared the LORD; and the creditor has come to take my two children to be his slaves'"* (2 Kings 4:1).

This woman was in a covenant relationship with God. When her husband Obed was alive, they had mortgaged their home to shelter and feed 100 prophets Jezebel sought to kill. She knew her rights under the covenant, including the promise from Proverbs 19:17: *"Those who lend to the Lord, he will repay."* With confidence in God's justice, she made her request. She was on the right side of right; she had sacrificed for the kingdom, and she knew God was a fair, generous, and compassionate judge. She made her ASK, her DEMAND—a demand rooted in faith.

So Elisha replied to her, "What shall I do for you?" She replied, "Your servant has nothing in the house except a jar of oil." Elisha instructed her, "Go, borrow containers elsewhere for yourself, empty containers from all your neighbors—do not get *too* few. Then you shall come in and shut the door behind you and your sons, and pour into all these containers; and you shall set aside what is full."

She obeyed without hesitation. She and her sons gathered containers, and the oil flowed until every container was full. When she reported back to Elisha, he said, *"Go, sell the oil and pay your debt; you and your sons can live on what is left"* (2 Kings 4:2-5, 7).

So, what do you need from God today? Clarify your request in prayer, write it down, and ask yourself, "Is my request aligned with God's will?" If it is, approach boldly and make your demand. Then, be ready to act on the instructions you receive. Like the widow, your obedience could lead to the miracle you need.

GENEROSITY BIRTHS MIRACLES

"Give and it shall be given back to you, but with increase. That's the Law of Giving."
~Scott Hogle

Desperate people make demands. In the early months of Covid, during shelter-in-place, I needed a miracle of money. Like the widow making a demand through Elisha, I was about to make a demand of God. Like her, I was about to tap into a promise of God; I needed help. Many businesses stopped advertising. As the Senior Vice President of Sales for iHeartMedia, my team and I faced a huge challenge. When businesses stopped advertising, salespeople stopped making commission. I had Account Executives receiving little or even zero pay. I became very troubled and went to God in prayer to ASK (make my demand) for help. God answers with ideas and instructions when we go to Him and ask for wisdom. So I asked with great expectation and believed He would answer me. I asked, "Lord, what shall I do?" God answered immediately, "Give it away." It took a couple of days for me to understand that it meant giving away the advertising. "What a ridiculous answer," I thought to myself. That won't help us; salespeople need to make commission. I can't do that; they will fire me if I give advertising away. So, I explained to the Lord how the advertising and sales compensation system works. Just kidding. After thinking about this for a few days, I realized I had nothing to lose in giving away public service announcements during a national crisis, letting people know which local businesses were still open and where they could purchase goods and services. I thought of turning our outside sales team into an outbound call center. Months later, something amazing happened. Many of the businesses that we gave free advertising to during the Covid crisis came back to us and became long-term annual clients worth millions of dollars in advertising revenue. God's answer to me required that I ACTIVATE my faith, TRUST in Him, and STAND on His promise found in Luke 6:38. It is God's guarantee that stipulates, *"Give and it shall be given, but when it is given back to you it will be returned with increase."* When you activate a promise of God, you tap into the covenant of grace whereby He provides all that you need. In fact, He doesn't just provide what you need; He provides <u>more than enough</u>.

MAKE YOUR ASK, THEN START SEEKING

*"Now to Him who is able to do far more abundantly beyond
all that we ask or think, according to the power that works
within us." Ephesians 3:20*

SEEK means to search, to HUNT until you find what you're looking for. When you're searching, there's an expectation of discovery. This is crucial in exercising your faith because you cannot receive what you do not expect. Your expectations shape your experiences. If you're not expecting the miraculous, a miracle could happen right before your eyes, and you'd miss it.

In my bestselling devotional *Divine Intelligence*, there's a chapter titled "The Puzzle Master." The principle is simple: God uses people as a piece to your puzzle to answer your prayer. In the same way, you are a piece of someone else's puzzle, used by God to answer their prayer. Whenever I am in need, the first question I ask myself is, "Where or in whom has God placed my answer?" Everything God does is through a person or place, so when I make my ASK of God, I am looking for an idea or instruction that will lead me to a person or place to find what I SEEK.

I was in a desperate situation, much like the widow, so I marched boldly into the Throne Room of Grace and made my case. And wow, did God ever answer! Just as Elisha asked the widow what she had and then used it to create a multiplication miracle, God led me to use what I had to create multiplication in my situation.

*"And you will seek Me and find Me when you search for Me
with all your heart."* Jeremiah 29:13

Do you know what part God wants you to play in your miracle? The instruction Elisha gave to the widow and the instruction God gave to me were critical for making way for God to do the miracle. If the widow had not done what Elisha asked, or if I had ignored God's instruction because it made no sense, then neither of us would have received our miracle. It seems counterintuitive, but God uses what we lack to create a miracle. Think of the farmer who discovered his **Acres of Diamonds** by realizing that the treasure he sought was right beneath his feet all along. Similarly, you need to recognize what God has already placed in your life to create your own miracle of multiplication.

So, let me ask you: **"What do you have in your house?"** Take a moment to carefully inventory everything you possess—not just the physical items, but also the intangible gifts you carry within—your talents, your abilities, your unique qualities. Then, seek God's guidance on how He wants to use these gifts. You might be amazed at how He can take the ordinary and transform it into the extraordinary through you.

But remember, the act of knocking requires action. It's about stepping forward and taking that leap of faith. No one can do your part except you. So often, people miss out on God's miracles because they ask, God answers, but then they fail to act.

In Daniel 9:23, we see that when we seek God and make our requests in prayer, His response is set in motion from the moment we pray: *"As soon as you began to pray, a word went out, which I have come to tell you, for you are highly esteemed"* (NIV). Daniel was earnestly seeking God, even fasting to ensure his spirit was attuned to whatever God might reveal. He also stood on a covenant promise given through the prophet Jeremiah: *"You will seek Me and find Me when you search for Me with all your heart"* (Jeremiah 29:13).

So, like Daniel, lean on God's promises, take action, and be ready for the miracle He will work through you. Your step of faith could be the very key that unlocks the miracles in your life and the lives of others through you.

REFLECT TO CONNECT

1. In what areas of your life do you sense a call to Ask, Seek, or Knock? How are you responding to that prompting?

2. How are you actively seeking God's presence, and how might you recognize the ways He's already providing in your life?

3. What personal significance does the Scripture, "Seek ye first the kingdom of heaven, and all these things shall be added unto you," hold for you? How does it influence your priorities and choices?

In Pursuit of the Divine

"As the deer panteth after the water brooks, so panteth my soul after thee, O God" Psalm 42:1 (KJV).

I have been pursuing God since my late teens and remember praying that God would give me a heart after His. At 17, I knew my heart was prone to drifting, so I asked God to give me an insatiable appetite for His word. I asked for a heart after His own heart, and He answered, but the answer came over time. While pursuing God in my business life, I realized there was a big disconnect between Sunday worship and Monday work. Lessons taught in church were limited in helping me with my work life. This disconnect pushed me to find ways to bring Jesus into my everyday everythings. Colossians 3:17 tells us: *"Whatever you do in word or deed, do everything in the name of the Lord Jesus, giving thanks through Him to God the Father."* In simple ways, I would discover that God was eager to be invited into every aspect of my life, no matter how small.

In my early 20s, as I started making sales calls, I would take a moment to pray in my car before meeting with clients. I asked God to guide me with the right questions and to grant me favor with the customer—and He did. Anything I invited God into became better with Him. I have discovered the truth of Matthew 6:33: *"Seek ye first the kingdom of God, and all these things shall be added unto you."* When you put God first, He blesses what you do.

How do you pursue God? For me, it started with recognizing my deep need for God and inviting Him to help in my everyday life. "Lord, how do I do xyz?" I was never afraid to ask. Involving God in your daily life is not only powerful—it's also something that pleases Him. As God walked with Adam in the garden during the cool of the day, so He desires to walk with you through your day. Pursuing God one day per week at church isn't enough for me. I want to read about Him and hear from Him in the morning, walk with Him in the midday, and think on Him before I turn in at night. My pursuit is not a destination I ever arrive at but a passion I practice. The joy is in the journey, and God rewards your passion to pursue Him. He says, *"God is a rewarder of those who diligently seek him"* (Hebrews 11:6). Here are three ideas you can use to pursue God and be filled with the Spirit as you go through your day.

1. **PURSUING GOD AT WORK:** One of my heroes of the faith was a monk named Brother Lawrence, who lived in a French Monastery in the 17th century. He modeled how to bring God into the simplest tasks as he went about his day. A book written about Brother Lawrence, *Practicing the Presence of God*, changed my life. Brother Lawrence did not distinguish his daily chores from his time of daily devotions. While working, he meditated on the goodness of God, giving thanks and reciting Scripture in his mind. He was able to experience God's presence 24/7. When his heart

drifted during the day, he did not condemn himself. He simply returned to "thinking on God" as often as he could. You, too, have the ability to multi-task in the spirit. While you are occupied with the duties of the day, you, too, can recalibrate your heart into a posture of devotion and appreciation toward God.

> *"My chief aim is to discover God in everything I do*
> *and enjoy him every minute of every day."*
> ~Scott Hogle

Decades later, my pursuit of the Divine would lead me to write the international bestseller *Divine Intelligence, How to Discover God In Your Work Life.* This daily devotional illustrates how to close the gap between work and worship. Your work becomes your worship when you dedicate it to the Lord. *Divine Intelligence* connects the dots between a simple Scripture for the day and God's strategy to succeed. Could anything be more practical? There can be no higher calling than to discover God in all that you do and then dedicate your daily doings to Him. This has been my pursuit of the Divine for longer than I can remember.

2. **PURSUING GOD IN QUESTIONS:** Do you inquire of the Lord? For me, no matter how close I am to God, I still feel the jolt when there is bad news. So, I have to remind myself to take a step back, take a breath, and remember Who is in control. After gathering my bearings, I say to myself, "God is never surprised by what surprised me." The bad news of today may have been

bad news for me, but it wasn't new news for God. God's got a plan; He's not sitting up in heaven wringing His hands, trying to figure out what to do. I just need to sit with Him to figure out His plan for my situation.

"And David inquired of the Lord." 1 Samuel 30:8

If you had to think back to the best advice you've ever gotten, what was it? Did it come from a parent, grandparent, teacher, coach, boss, friend, or mentor? Bob Beaudine would tell you that for him, it came from his mother, Martha. Just before Bob graduated from college, Martha shared what she called "a secret" that had been passed down to her. That secret was that God wanted to spend time with him every day to guide him with strategic counsel for the things he would face. Following his mother's advice, Bob set up two chairs in his home and has been meeting there with God ever since. He credits all his success to this daily meeting. Bob Beaudine learned to ask three questions, and when I think on them, they too, RECENTER me with the presence of God. In Bob Beaudine's national bestselling book *2 Chairs: The Secret that Changes Everything,* he lists three questions that have helped me to REFRAME my thinking whenever I am facing a crisis.

- DOES GOD KNOW MY SITUATION? (The answer to this is, "Of course He does.")
- IS IT TOO HARD FOR HIM? (The answer to this is, "Of course it's not.")
- DOES HE HAVE A GOOD PLAN FOR ME? (The answer to this is, "Of course He does.")

These questions help me to seek God's perspective, look for His purpose in the situation, and wait for His plan to emerge so I can navigate the crisis.

3. **PURSUING GOD IN WORSHIP:** One of the simple ways I experience God's presence during my day is while walking the hallways at work. Whether it's just before or after lunch, I practice what I call "The Art of the Promise Walker." For every season of life, there's a theme song, and for every season, there's a scripture that offers strength. As I move from one place to another, I redeem those micro-moments by reciting the Scriptures God has given me for the season. I encourage you to do the same. Find a few Scriptures that resonate with where you are right now. Keep them close—in your heart or even in your notes on your phone—and let them refresh you throughout your day. And if you can find a few moments for worship as you walk from your car to your office or as you move from place to place, remember this: you're just a few verses away from stepping into God's presence. Here are 7 Scriptures of Strength that encourage me on my promise walks.

   1. *"I will come down and speak with you there."* Numbers 11:17
   2. *"I will instruct you and teach you in the way you should go; I will counsel you with my loving eye on you."* Psalm 32:8

3. *"He that dwelleth in the secret place of the most High shall abide under the shadow of the Almighty."* Psalm 91:1

4. *"Call to Me, and I will answer you and tell you great and mighty things which you do not know."* Ref. Jeremiah 33:3, AMP

5. *"I have told you these things so that in Me you may have peace. In this world you will have trouble. But take heart! I have overcome the world."* John 16:33

6. *"But when He, the Spirit of truth, comes, He will guide you into all the truth; for He will not speak on His own, but whatever He hears, He will speak, and He will disclose to you what is to come."* John 16:13

7. *"Remain in Me, and I in you. Just as the branch cannot bear fruit of itself but must remain in the vine, so neither can you unless you remain in Me."* John 15:4

REFLECT TO CONNECT

1. In what ways do you pursue God?
2. What one question would you like to ask God today?
3. Do you wait on God for answers or do you play ding-dong ditch?

The Difference Maker

*"Truly I say to you, to the extent that you did it
for one of the least of these brothers or sisters of Mine,
you did it for Me"* Matthew 25:40.

Making a living is essential, but making a difference is eternal. While our needs push us to earn an income, our souls yearn to make an impact. There's a God-sized void in our hearts that can only be filled by serving Christ. This void acts as a beacon, drawing us toward a life that rises above the daily grind and touches the eternal. Our definition of growth and success often differs from God's. We tend to measure success by the outcomes and the return on investment, but God calls us to focus on the eternal, to live as temporary citizens passing through this world on our journey to the next. So, how do you define growth? How do you define success? Who are you becoming as you move from the temporary toward the eternal? Are you growing in Christ and using what God has entrusted to you for a higher purpose? If so, you're walking in your Divine Destiny.

What are you living for today that will outlive you? In my pursuit of prosperity early in my career, there came a point in time when making a living wasn't enough; I longed to make a difference. While I still needed to earn a living, my heart wasn't satisfied and craved something more. Making a difference meant living for a higher purpose, one that went beyond earning a paycheck. In my 20s, success was enough, but in my 30s, I needed significance. John Maxwell, the world's foremost expert on leadership, defined success as "adding value to oneself, but significance is adding value to others." I have discovered that to be true. After years of chasing success for myself, something shifted—I felt a deep desire to make a difference by helping others. This wasn't limited to serving in church; it extended to my everyday work as a broadcaster. I realized I could help others in their careers and callings right where I was. In the process of adding value to others, I found true significance.

Over time, I began to ask myself defining questions: "What am I doing in my work life to make a difference? Is my focus on things that will have eternal impact, or am I chasing things with temporal benefits?"

How would you answer these questions for yourself?

Success and significance are both important; one can be a step toward the other. Significance, which is adding value to others, will increase your influence. Success, which involves adding value to yourself, can provide income you can use to make a difference. The Gospel is free, but not the cost to evangelize. Serving others often means providing for them in some fashion. As you pursue your Divine Destiny, here are a few differences between success and significance to keep in mind.

SEASONS OF GROWTH

"Success leaves a God-size hole in your heart that only significance can fill."

SUCCESS	SIGNIFICANCE
Destination focused	Journey oriented
Adds value to self	Adds value to others
Focused on building a life	Focused on building a legacy
Wants to compete with others	Desires to complete others
Creates success milestones	Creates eternal stepping stones
Can leave a hole in your heart	Can satisfy an ache in your soul

SERVE WHERE YOU ARE AT, THEN OCCUPY

"Brothers and sisters, each one is to remain with God in that condition in which he was called; Occupy until I come."
1 Corinthians 7:24 & Luke 19:13

You can make a difference right where you are at. Making a difference starts right where you are. Investing in eternity means serving God and people, whether you're in the marketplace or ministry. Serving God's purpose where you are is your HIGH CALL. The very need, pain point, or desire that your spirit is attuned to is where you'll find God's purpose for you in this season. Your Divine Destiny is to address the need in front of you, solve the problems you and others face, and care for the least of these, just as Jesus spoke of in Matthew 25. Serving Jesus does not mean you should quit your job. On the contrary, you are called where you are in this season for a reason. God needs as many people working vocationally in the marketplace as in the ministry. You can serve God just as effectively in the marketplace as a minister can working in a church. In fact, one of heaven's greatest needs is to have godly men and women working in government, finance, health care, etc. Before leaving Earth, Jesus told his disciples, "OCCUPY UNTIL I COME," which means to trade and do business. He wanted them to serve Him but also to get on with life. Don't sit on the bench while waiting for His return; get busy serving YOUR eternal purpose, your Divine Destiny, your high call. If you desire to start investing in eternity but don't know where to start, start with the need in front of you.

BECOMING A DIFFERENCE-MAKER

Where do I start? Mother Teressa was once asked how to change the world, and she replied, "Start with the person in front of you." That's how you become a difference-maker. Jesus went as far as to say that when we serve others, He credits our service as if we are serving Him directly. By becoming the hands and feet of Jesus, we are serving a higher purpose: His purpose. By embracing Jesus's definition of success and significance, we begin to live with an eternal perspective in this life. Jesus said, *"Then the King will say to those on His right, 'Come, you who are blessed of My Father, inherit the kingdom prepared for you from the foundation of the world. For I was hungry, and you gave Me something to eat; I was thirsty, and you gave Me something to drink; I was a stranger, and you invited Me in; naked, and you clothed Me; I was sick, and you visited Me; I was in prison, and you came to Me.' Then the righteous will answer Him, 'Lord, when did we see You hungry, and feed You, or thirsty, and give You something to* *drink? And when did we see You as a stranger, and invite You in, or naked, and clothe You? And when did we see You sick, or in prison, and come to You?' And the King will answer and say to them, 'Truly I say to you, to the extent that you did it for one of the least of these brothers or sisters of Mine, you did it for Me'"* (Matthew 25:34-40). Your Divine Destiny is letting Christ shine through you as you journey with Him toward eternity.

 **REFLECT TO CONNECT:**

1. What need around you stirs your heart and captures your attention?
2. Is there a person, place, or purpose that keeps drawing you in, urging you to take action?
3. What have you been avoiding that your inner voice continues to nudge you about?

ABOUT THE AUTHOR

SCOTT HOGLE is a thirty-year career broadcaster, president of iHeartMedia Honolulu, bestselling author of the business book *Persuade* and the fifty-two-week devotional *Divine Intelligence*, a founding member of The John Maxwell Team, and a licensed teaching pastor at New Hope Oahu. Scott is married to Kate Hogle, and they live in Honolulu, Hawaii, with their two sons, Bailey and Casey.